ARTHUR MILLER

Literature and Life: American Writers

Selected list of titles in the series:

Complete list of titles in the series available from the publisher on request.

ARTHUR MILLER

June Schlueter
and
James K. Flanagan

UNGAR • NEW YORK

1987

The Ungar Publishing Company
370 Lexington Avenue, New York, N.Y. 10017

Printed in the United States of America

Library of Congress Cataloging-in-Publication Data

Schlueter, June.
    Arthur Miller.

    (Literature and life. American writers)
    Bibliography: p.
    Includes index.
    1. Miller, Arthur, 1915–   —Criticism and
interpretation. I. Flanagan, James K. II. Title.
III. Series.
PS3525.I5156Z88 1987   812'.52   87-5991
ISBN 0-8044-2797-6

Acknowledgments will be found on page 165,
which constitutes an extension of the copyright page.

Contents

Authors' Note

The division of labor on this book is perhaps clearer than with most collaborations: Flanagan prepared the Chronology and wrote the introductory biographical chapter "Literature and Life." Schlueter wrote the critical analyses of the plays, though small portions of the chapters on *The Crucible, A View from the Bridge*, and *After the Fall* rely on commentary in Flanagan's 1969 dissertation on Miller.

Chronology

1915   Arthur Miller is born October 17 on East 112th Street in Harlem, the second child of Isadore (a manufacturer of women's clothing) and Augusta Barnett Miller. The elder son, Kermit, will be the model for the older brother in several of his brother's plays.

1921   A sister, Joan, is born, later to become an actress with the stage name Joan Copeland.

1928   After the family business fails, the Millers move to Schermerhorn Street in the Midwood section of Brooklyn, where other relatives between jobs and Grandfather Barnett, who lives in six-month shifts at various daughters' homes, stay temporarily. Both Arthur's grandfather and father are sources for several of his blunt, tough father characters. Arthur attends James Madison High School. More an athlete than a scholar, he receives an injury in a football game later to keep him out of military service and works for a bakery, rising at 4:00 A.M. to deliver bread and rolls.

1930   Miller transfers to Abraham Lincoln High School, nearer to his home.

1933   He graduates from high school, discovers reading through Dostoevsky's *The Brothers Karamazov*. When he applies to the University of Michigan, he is refused admission because he has failed algebra three times, has been expelled from class on several occasions, and has been unable to get recommendations from his teachers.

He temporarily works for his father in a newly established garment firm, but he comes quickly to hate the business. As a result, he writes a never-published short story, "In Memoriam," about the difficult life of a salesman and looks for something else. He also works briefly at a small Brooklyn radio station as a crooner, then gets a job in an auto parts warehouse in Manhattan.

1934–39 He enters the University of Michigan after writing the dean that he was "a much more serious fellow." While in college, he meets Mary Grace Slattery, who will be his first wife. He studies playwriting under Professor Kenneth Rowe and wins two Avery Hopwood Awards: in 1936 for *No Villain* and in 1937 for *Honors at Dawn*. In 1938, his senior year, he wins the Theater Guild National Award for *They Too Arise* (a revision of *No Villain*, revised again that year as *The Grass Still Grows*) and writes another play, *The Great Disobedience*. Upon graduation, he returns to New York, where he participates in the New York Federal Theater Project, coauthoring a play with Norman Rosten entitled *Listen My Children* (1939).

1940 After the Federal Theater Project is abolished, Miller goes on relief; he completes *The Golden Years*. On August 5, he marries Mary Grace Slattery, who works as a waitress and as an editor so Miller can write.

1941 Two radio scripts are completed: *The Pussycat and the Expert Plumber Who Was a Man* and *William Ireland's Confession*. He also works in a box factory, as a scriptwriter in bond drives, and as a shipfitter's helper at the Brooklyn Navy Yard.

1942 He writes *The Four Freedoms*, a radio play.

1943 Work on *The Half-Bridge*, begun in 1941, is completed. He demonstrates an interest in Marxism and attends a study course in a vacant store in Brooklyn. In December, *That They May Win*, his one-act support-the-war-effort play, is produced by a community group in Brooklyn.

1944   September 7, a daughter, Jane, is born. After reading Ernie Pyle's *Here Is Your War*, he visits army camps across the country for background material for his screenplay, *The Story of G. I. Joe*, and his book of military reportage, *Situation Normal*. His first Broadway production, *The Man Who Had All the Luck*, closes in November after six performances and is published in *Cross-Section: A Collection of New American Writing*.

1945   He publishes *Focus*, a novel about anti-Semitism; a radio play, *Grandpa and the Statue*; and *That They May Win*. In an article in *New Masses* magazine, he attacks Ezra Pound for his profascist activism.

1946   In April, "The Plaster Masks," a short story, receives national circulation in *Encore: A Continuing Anthology Nine*.

1947   May 31, a son, Robert, is born. *All My Sons*, his first success, opens on Broadway in January. Miller's name appears in an ad in the *Daily Worker* protesting the treatment of German antifascist refugees like Gerhard Eisler. He auctions off the manuscript of *All My Sons* in behalf of the Progressive Citizens of America, and his name appears as a sponsor of the World Youth Festival under the aegis of the communist-dominated World Federation of Democratic Youth in Prague. "It Takes a Thief" appears in *Collier's* in February; *The Story of Gus* is included in *Radio's Best Plays*, his adaptation of Ferenc Molnar's *The Guardsman* in *Theater Guild on the Air*; on June 22, he publishes an essay, "Subsidized Theater," in the *New York Times*.

1949   In February, *Death of a Salesman* opens on Broadway

xii Arthur Miller

and goes on to win the New York Drama Critics Circle Award and the Pulitzer Prize; the same month, Miller publishes "Tragedy and the Common Man," and in March "Arthur Miller on 'The Nature of Tragedy'" in the *New York Times*, the first of many essays on drama, the theater, politics, and human rights to appear in the years to come.

1950   He meets Marilyn Monroe at Twentieth Century-Fox Studios. *Death of a Salesman* closes in November after a run of 742 performances. His version of Ibsen's *An Enemy of the People* opens in December and runs for thirty-six performances.

1951   Miller begins leading a social life without his wife. He publishes *An Enemy of the People* and, in *Harper's*, "Monte Saint Angelo," a short story; he writes a screenplay, *The Hook*.

1953   *The Crucible* opens on Broadway and evokes mixed reviews that differ strongly about the play's relevance to McCarthyism.

1954   Marilyn Monroe is divorced from Joe DiMaggio.

1955   At a party in May, Miller and Monroe meet again, recognizing a strong mutual attraction. In June, Miller contracts to write a film script for the New York City Youth Board, but after he is attacked for leftist connections in the *New York Herald-Tribune*, he is dropped from the film. The one-act version of *A View from the Bridge* and *A Memory of Two Mondays* opens in September and runs for 149 performances.

1956   He is divorced from Mary Grace Slattery and in June marries Marilyn Monroe, the same month he is subpoenaed to appear before the HUAC; he refuses to name names and is cited for contempt of Congress. The two-act version of *A View from the Bridge* opens in London in October for a run of 220 performances.

1957   In May, he is convicted of contempt of Congress and finds himself blacklisted. "The Misfits," a short story, appears in *Esquire*. Marilyn, pregnant, loses the child late in the year, resulting in serious depression that will last until her death; Miller reworks "The Misfits" into a screenplay for her. He publishes *Collected Plays*.

1958   *The Misfits* is filmed with Marilyn starring as Roslyn. In August, the US Court of Appeals for the District of Columbia reverses Miller's contempt conviction.

1959   In December, *Esquire* publishes a short story, "I Don't Need You Any More."

1960   "Please Don't Kill Anything," a short story, appears in *Noble Savage*.

1961   Marilyn Monroe applies for a Mexican divorce in January. In March, Miller's mother dies. *Redbook* reprints "Please Don't Kill Anything"; *Esquire* publishes "The Prophecy." *Uno Sguardo dal Ponte*, operatic version of *A View from the Bridge*, by Renzo Rossellini, premieres in Rome. The New York City Opera Company puts on Robert Ward's version of *The Crucible*.

1962   In February, Miller marries Ingeborg Morath, a photographer for Magnum. In August, Marilyn Monroe commits suicide. *Noble Savage* publishes "Glimpse at a Jockey."

1963   Miller begins work on *After the Fall* and publishes a children's story, *Jane's Blanket*. In September, a daughter, Rebecca (named after Miller's mother), is born.

1964   *After the Fall* opens in January at the ANTA-Washing-

xiv Arthur

ton Square Theatre and is performed by the Lincoln Center Repertory Theater but is immediately criticized as being too obviously confessional. In March, he is special commentator for the *New York Herald-Tribune* at the Nazi trials at Frankfurt, Germany. In December, *Incident at Vichy* opens at Lincoln Center.

1965   *Incident at Vichy* is published. Miller is elected president of International PEN.

1966   *Death of a Salesman* is presented on CBS to an audience of seventeen million; *Esquire* publishes "The Recognitions"; the *Saturday Evening Post* publishes "Search for a Future."

1967   He publishes a collection of nine short stories entitled *I Don't Need You Any More*. In April, *The Crucible* is presented by CBS. In October, *Uno Sguardo dal Ponte* premieres in America at the Philadelphia Lyric Opera.

1968   *The Price* opens on Broadway in February and the millionth copy of *Death of a Salesman* is sold in March. Miller attends the Democratic National Convention in Chicago as a Eugene McCarthy delegate. He petitions the Soviet government to lift the ban on the works of Aleksandr Solzhenitsyn.

1969   *The Price* closes in February, after 425 performances. Miller refuses to allow his works to be published in Greece in protest of that government's oppression of writers. In September, he retires as president of International PEN. *The Reason Why*, an antiwar allegory of Miller's, is filmed on his Connecticut farm. With Inge Morath, he publishes *In Russia* in November.

1970   In February, he supports a Roxbury high school teacher who refuses to say the Pledge of Allegiance in her classroom. Brandeis University honors him with a Creative

Arts Award Medal in May. In November, two one-act plays, *Fame* and *The Reason Why*, run for twenty performances at New York's New Theater Workshop. At the end of the year, the Soviet Union, reacting to *In Russia* and to his advocacy of freedom for writers, bans all of Miller's works.

1971   In February, *The Price* appears on ABC-TV and *A Memory of Two Mondays* is presented by PBS. In March, his version of Ibsen's *An Enemy of the People* opens at Lincoln Center for a short run. With Miller's help, the Brazilian playwright Augusto Boal is freed from prison and visits the US. In December, Miller is elected to the American Academy of Arts and Letters. *The Portable Arthur Miller*, a collection of writings edited by Harold Clurman, is published.

1972   In February, Miller attacks the three-year sentence imposed on publisher Ralph Ginzburg for a 1963 obscenity conviction upheld by the US Supreme Court in a five-to-four decision. The next month, he also protests the barring of four Cuban film directors from the US and, in Russia, the dismissal of Valery Panov from the Kirov State Dance Theater for requesting to emigrate. In April, he gives permission for an all-black *Death of a Salesman* production in Baltimore; *The Crucible* is revived at Lincoln Center, but Miller criticizes the center's board of directors for mismanagement. He reviews *In Hiding*, by Ronald Fraser, a book about Manuel Cortes, who hid thirty years in his own house to escape death under the Franco regime. In November, *The Creation of the World and Other Business*, a comedy, opens to bad reviews and closes after only twenty performances.

1973   *The Creation of the World and Other Business* is published. Miller is appointed adjunct professor in residence at the University of Michigan for the academic year 1973–74, where his students work on performing

scenes from *The American Clock*. In November, by permitting the Philadelphia Drama Guild to mount *Death
of a Salesman*, he allows the play to be performed for
the first time since 1949 within less than a hundred
miles of Broadway.

1974   In January, Miller and others urge the UN to proclaim
1974 as "World Amnesty Year." At Michigan in April,
he produces a revised version of *The Creation of the
World and Other Business*. CBS-TV produces *After the
Fall* in December.

1975   Miller brings *Death of a Salesman* back to New York in
June but at the Circle in the Square instead of on Broadway. Throughout the year he is active in public denunci-
ation of UNESCO's resolutions and actions that seek to
isolate Israel. In August, he joins other literary figures to
protest the imprisonment and torture of writers in Iran
under the shah. Czech poet and playwright Pavel Kohout addresses an open letter to Miller and other noted
writers to assure their continuing help to further the
cause of human rights. In November, Miller appears
with a panel before the Senate Permanent Subcommittee
on Investigations to support the freedom of writers
throughout the world. In the same month, he joins
friends of Peter Reilly, convicted of murdering his mother in Canaan, Connecticut, in September 1973, to bring
about a new trial. Enlisting the help of the *New York
Times*, detectives of the Sixth Homicide Zone in
Harlem, and a private investigator, Miller helps bring
public pressure on the judicial system.

1976   In January, Miller participates in a symposium on Jewish culture in which he asserts that Jewish writers live in
an apocalyptic context and are all "dancing on the edge
of a precipice." *The Crucible* is produced at Stratford,
Connecticut, in June; *The Archbishop's Ceiling* is produced in New Haven. "Ham Sandwich," a fragment of a

short story, and *The Poosidin's Resignation*, a fragment
of a play, appear in *Boston University Quarterly*. In
November, charges against Peter Reilly are dropped.

1977   Oppressed Czech writers appeal to Miller for help from
government harassment. *In the Country*, with photographs by Inge Morath, is published in January. In February, Miller joins fifty-three other literary figures in a
letter to Czech head of state Gustav Husak protesting
the arrest of dissidents. *The Archbishop's Ceiling* opens
in April for a limited run at Washington's Kennedy Center to unsatisfactory reviews.

1978   In July, Miller is part of a protest march and rally near
the Soviet Mission to the UN concerning the arrests of
dissidents such as Aleksandr I. Ginzburg and Anatoly B.
Scheransky. In November, NBC produces the comedy
Fame to lukewarm reviews. In the same month, Miller
and his wife visit the People's Republic of China. *The
Theater Essays of Arthur Miller* is published.

1979   *The Price*, revived on Broadway in April, is a critical and
financial success. Miller writes the screenplay for Fania
Fenelon's *Playing for Time* and is criticized by the author and by many liberals for his defense of CBS's choice
of Vanessa Redgrave for the leading role. In October, he
participates in a march at the Czech UN Mission protesting violation of the 1975 Helsinki Accords. In November, a film entitled *Arthur Miller on Home Ground*
is shown at the Carnegie Hall Cinema in New York.
Chinese Encounters, with Inge Morath, is published.

1980   With Cao Yu, China's most respected dramatist, Miller
presents a program on "Theater in Modern China" at
Columbia University in March. In May, *The American
Clock* opens at Spoleto USA Festival at Charleston, SC,
to critical praise. In June, Miller signs a letter with other
American Jews protesting the Begin government's ex-

pansion of settlements on the West Bank. In August, he
joins with several other writers, including Edward Albee, John Updike, and Bernard Malamud, in a letter of
support for the Polish Solidarity movement. *Playing for
Time* is telecast on CBS in September; both Miller's
script and Redgrave's acting are praised. *The American
Clock*, with Miller's sister playing Rose Baum, based on
their mother, opens on Broadway in November and
closes after only twelve performances.

1981   In October, he narrates a concert version of *Up from
Paradise*, set to music by Stanley Silverman, at the Whit-
ney Museum in New York. He publishes *Collected
Plays, Volume Two*, and *Playing for Time*.

1982   Miller attempts unsuccessfully in March to save two
Broadway theaters from demolition. With other playwrights, he attacks a suit by Broadway producers to
limit dramatists' earnings. In October, *Elegy for a Lady*
and *Some Kind of Love Story* open at the Long Wharf
Theater in New Haven to unimpressive reviews, and
The American Clock is published.

1983   The successful revival of *A View from the Bridge* opens
in February on Broadway. The next month, Miller and
his wife travel to China to begin the production of *Death
of a Salesman* in Beijing. In May, Miller's greatest play
wins rare standing ovations from Chinese audiences;
while they are in China, a fire damages their Roxbury
home extensively. *Up from Paradise* is revised and revived off-Broadway in October at Manhattan's Jewish
Repertory Theater. In the same month, New York University announces that Miller is to be one of the recipi-
ents of its Bobst Award Medal and $2,500 stipend.

1984   He publishes *"Salesman" in Beijing*, with photographs
by Inge Morath, and a revised version of *The Archbishop's Ceiling*. *Death of a Salesman* is revived on Broadway in March and is successful both financially and

critically, but trouble occurs when Dustin Hoffman (Willy Loman) insists that the number of performances a week be reduced; producer Robert Whitehead, a longtime Miller associate, leaves the play; and Miller is angered by the omission of all the play's actors from the Tony nominations. In May, he and his wife are awarded honorary doctorates from the University of Hartford. At the end of the year, he is involved in a dispute with the experimental off-off-Broadway Wooster Group over their unauthorized use of scenes from *The Crucible* in a play entitled *L.S.D.*

1985   In January, a revival of *The Price* opens successfully on Broadway. Miller announces in February that he is writing his autobiography. In March, he contributes $50,000 to the Hopwood Visiting Writers Fund at the University of Michigan, then travels with Harold Pinter to Istanbul to lend solidarity to Turkish writers. In September, *Death of a Salesman*, with Dustin Hoffman as Willy, is aired by CBS and seen by an audience of twenty-five million. In October, Miller reads from his work at PEN Celebration; later that month, he takes a stand on an immigration law that denies permanent residence to certain artists.

1986   *The Crucible* is revived at Trinity Repertory Company in New York, *All My Sons* at the Long Wharf Theatre in Connecticut. In London, there are productions of *The American Clock* and *The Archbishop's Ceiling*. Miller publishes *Danger: Memory!*, consisting of two one-act plays, *I Don't Remember Anything* and *Clara*.

1987   In January, Public Television airs a revival of *All My Sons*, with James Whitmore. In February, *Danger: Memory!* opens at the Mitzi E. Newhouse Theater, Lincoln Center. In April, a revival of *All My Sons* appears on Broadway, winning a Tony award. Miller's autobiography, *Timebends: A Life*, is scheduled for November publication by Grove Press.

1

Arthur Miller:
Literature and Life

If I have had a life at all worth mentioning,
it is in my plays.[1]

Arthur Miller was born on October 17, 1915, on East 112th Street
in Manhattan to Isadore and Augusta Barnett Miller. His father, like
many late nineteenth century immigrant Jews, had entered the garment business in New York City and was, at the time of Arthur's
birth, a manufacturer of women's clothing. Arthur was the second
of three children; Kermit, the oldest by several years, is a salesman,
and Joan, born in 1921, appears on stage under the professional
name of Joan Copeland. The Millers lived in Manhattan but were
forced to move to Schermerhorn Street in the Midwood section of
Brooklyn when the family manufacturing firm failed in 1928 during
the early stages of the Depression.

Miller found the change from the swarming streets of Manhattan to the almost rural atmosphere of Brooklyn to be a move to a
different world: it was his first experience with a social unit larger
than the family but nevertheless still small enough to comprehend.
In marked contrast to the unending streets and crowds of Manhattan, Brooklyn suggested self-containment and a spirit of community identity. In his recollections of these times, Miller speaks of a
sense of harmony and interdependence between the family and the
neighborhood, casting Brooklyn as an island of peace and stability
in a time of social and economic confusion.[2]

For Miller's family, and for the men especially, a happy life
meant that business was running smoothly. However, the impact of
the Depression was powerful on real as well as fictional characters.

1

For Miller, the Depression and its significance not only indicated the dependence of the family upon outside support but also made him aware of a plane of life where men struggled with issues beyond those of raising a family.

Miller translates this social consciousness into one of his basic literary tenets: "that public issues be the congealing point of a writer's passions."[3] He might have added that such "passions" in his own writing seem to work toward an understanding of the forces that move and disrupt lives. In "The Shadows of the Gods," he speaks of how, until 1929, he believed in a prevailing design. When the Bank of the United States closed and people lined up outside it, he thought himself immuned from the exigencies of the economy, having withdrawn his twelve-dollar savings the day before. The youth went ahead with his plan to purchase a racing bike, but when it was stolen later that week, he understood that no one could escape the national disaster.[4]

It would be mistaken, however, to attribute to Miller's youth such a perceptive and articulate awareness of his social environment. His conscious interests were of a different order. During this time, Miller attended James Madison High School, located more than three miles from his home. He was an athlete, often trotting the distance to school to keep in shape. The hierarchy of values that his adolescent world held were like those of the Loman brothers in *Death of a Salesman*, primarily physical and athletic, those of the mind being quite unimportant. Miller could recall no intellectuals among his group of friends, only boys working to make the team or physically to excel.[5]

There was a darker side to his youthful activities: an injured back suffered in a football game, later to keep him from military service, curtailed his participation in sports. And the Depression meant that Arthur must get a job to help in the survival of the family, rising at four in the morning and delivering rolls and bread for a neighborhood bakery.

Midway through his high school career, Miller transferred to Abraham Lincoln High School, closer to his home, from which he was graduated in 1932. His senior year was anything but successful scholastically; however, like young Bert in *A Memory of Two Mon-*

days (1955), who reads Tolstoy's *War and Peace* on the subway, Miller became interested in a Russian novel, Dostoevsky's *The Brothers Karamazov*. It was his awakening to the power of literature: "There was an invisible world of cause and effect, mysterious, full of surprises, implacable in its course."[6] Miller's recognition of the intellectual life was so late that his attempts to enroll in college were in vain, even after the University of Michigan agreed to reconsider his application if he obtained four letters of recommendation from his teachers indicating at least some maturity in academic matters in his final year. But since he had flunked algebra three times, had on several occasions been expelled from class, and was not considered a promising student by most of his teachers, he did not receive the letters. The only alternative was work. Miller at first tried working with his father, who was attempting to establish another garment firm. He came to hate the coat business, especially the almost inhuman treatment of salesmen by the brusque, arrogant, often crude buyers. At this time, Miller recorded his sympathy for the difficult life of a salesman in a short story, "In Memoriam," which he filed away in a trunk, where his mother found it in 1949.[7] This admittedly abortive attempt was the first formal step toward the development of the world's most famous salesman, Willy Loman.

From the garment district, Miller moved to radio, where he tried crooning for several months over a small Brooklyn radio station, and, finally, like Bert in *A Memory of Two Mondays*, to an auto-parts warehouse in Manhattan, where he saved his money to reapply for college.

It was the Depression, 1932. Miller recalls what his new life entailed:

An invisible vise seemed to be forever closing tighter and tighter, and the worst, most unimaginable fates became ordinary. The star football player became a shipping clerk, and was glad to have the job; I, who had planned to go to Cornell because they offered a free course in biology—although I had not the slightest interest in the subject waited around until the fall term began, and seeing that nobody in the house was in possession of the fare, I went to the employment offices for a couple of months and ended up in a warehouse.[8]

Miller's desire to go to college persisted. Twice the University of Michigan turned him down because of his poor academic record. But a letter from Miller finally convinced the dean that he was ready to become a serious student, and the University admitted him. Miller entered Michigan at a time when the uncertainties of life held the upper hand everywhere. He first studied economics, then history, and was disappointed with both. He developed a strong aversion to any institution—economic, political, academic, or theological—that claims sole possession of the truth. The combination of skepticism and cynicism that such a viewpoint engenders persists throughout Miller's writing. Capitalism, the academic life, the Puritan ethos, the American political system are institutions which, when they pretend to represent truth, become forces of destruction for several of Miller's heroes.

It was at this time that Miller began to read Ibsen, Chekhov, O'Neill, the Greeks, and the German Expressionists and to move toward formulating a concept of the writer's role. The Depression set the requirements for Miller's writing, generating impatience with art for art's sake. This burning social concern was also linked with a more pragmatic reason for Miller's decision to try playwriting. He chose the University of Michigan because it was hospitable to aspiring writers; the Avery Hopwood Awards given by the Theater Guild's Bureau of New Plays presented prizes ranging from $250 to $1,250 to undergraduate playwrights. Under Professor Kenneth Rowe of the English Department, Miller worked toward that goal.

Since playwriting was thrust upon him, in a sense as a means of survival, Miller's position was different from the stereotypical artist who chose poverty rather than sacrifice himself to the vulgar clutches of commercialism. Miller regarded these early efforts as necessary and pragmatic means to a serious and dedicated end: becoming a playwright.

In 1926, Miller won the Hopwood Award for *No Villain*, which deals with a conflict between a man who owns a small garment-making firm and his university-educated son, Arnold Simon, who is a socialist.[9] He won it again in 1937 for *Honors at Dawn*. A Depression-era period piece, set alternately in a factory and a university, the play treats conflicts within the Zabriski family and champions unionism-socialism over capitalism. In 1938, *They Too Arise*, a reworking of *No Villain* that emphasizes more fully the complexity of the conflict between familial and social values, failed to win the lucrative $1,250 Hopwood senior award, but it won the Theater Guild award, which also paid $1,250.[10]

In these three early plays, Miller's protagonists are young men who believe in the purity of a cause. Reflecting the fledgling writer's major social and political concerns while he was in college, the University of Michigan plays are committed to movements (communism in *No Villain*, unionism in *Honors at Dawn*, socialism in *They Too Arise*) that result in oversimplified visions and drama. The conflict drawn in all three is typical of the propagandistic American drama of the 1930s, where characters are types, the source of injustice is readily located, and the message is of highest importance. In all three plays, the protagonist asserts his allegiance to the cause in a stirringly idealistic final scene but does not recognize that his mentality (us vs. them) reflects the same defensive attitude he abhors.

Miller revised *No Villain* for a second time in 1938, calling the reworking *The Grass Still Grows*, and wrote another play, *The Great Disobedience*, as well. In June 1938 he received his bachelor of arts degree and left Michigan to participate in the New York Federal Theater project. He hitchhiked to New York, as does Arnold Simon in *No Villain* and *They Too Arise*, with a young salesman, and on the way home Miller tried to express what his days at Ann Arbor had done for him:

> It was, in short, the testing ground for all my prejudices, my beliefs and my ignorance, and it helped me to lay out the boundaries for my life. For me it had, above everything else, variety and freedom.[11]

New York City was home and a place of hope for Miller. It was the center of artistic activity for the nation, where both on and off Broadway men like Martin Beck, Lee Shubert, and Guthrie McClintic were struggling to keep the theater alive in the Depression. The Roosevelt administration, through the WPA, sponsored the incorporation by Congress of the American National Theater and Academy (approved July 5, 1935), a nonprofit corporation, with no capital stock, to stimulate production and public interest in drama.

Miller's activity with the Federal Theater Project was limited to coauthoring a play, *Listen My Children*, an attack on the petty tyranny of governmental agencies, with Norman Rosten, who later did the screenplay for *A View from the Bridge*. Miller called it "a farcical sort of play about standing and waiting in a relief office. . . . It was a one-act sketch that was later amplified. Nothing ever came of it, I am glad to say."[12]

After the Federal Theater Project was abolished in 1939, Miller went on relief for a while, completed *The Golden Years* (1939–40), and wrote several radio scripts at one-hundred dollars each for *Columbia Workshop*, the *U.S. Steel Hour*, and *Cavalcade of America*. *The Pussy Cat and the Expert Plumber Who Was a Man*, one of these radio scripts, is an overly moralistic fable in which Tom, a talking cat, by liberally using blackmail and bribery, is awarded his party's nomination for governor. He is exposed before the election by Sam, a plumber and proletarian, who forces Tom to agree that, whereas a cat will do anything for physical comfort, a man may prefer to stay poor for an ideal. *William Ireland's Confession*, another radio script, is a literary ghost story in which Ireland returns from death to give an account of his Shakespearean forgeries; the piece ends with the voice of Shakespeare asking Ireland for help in rewriting *Hamlet*.[13]

While Miller was doing radio work, which he despised,[14] he married Mary Grace Slattery, whom he had met at the University of Michigan. For the next four years, from 1940–44, he worked at various jobs in a box factory, as a scriptwriter for bond drives, and as a shipfitter's helper on the swing shift in the Brooklyn Navy Yard. During this time, his wife worked as a waitress and as an editor at Harper & Brothers to enable him to write.

During the war years, Miller became strongly interested in Marxism. Speaking before the House Un-American Activities Committee in 1956, he recalled that he had attended a Marxist study course in a vacant store in his neighborhood in Brooklyn at the outset of World War II.[15] However, like the great majority of American intellectuals of those years, Miller's main concern was not so much with internal political problems as with the war against fascism that had to be won. His writings, such as *The Half-Bridge* (1941–43), reflect the patriotism and propaganda that were the sources of inspiration for the country.

On December 21, 1943, Miller saw the production of his one-act play *That They May Win*. Produced for the Victory Committee of Welfare Center 67 at Albermarle Road in Brooklyn, the play was mounted by Stage for Action, a "socially-minded dramatic group" devoted to helping society recognize that "the war, the peace, and their entire futures depend on what they themselves do—now."[16] A propaganda piece directed at coping with inflation by encouraging responsible citizenship, the play portrays the difficulties of a wounded war hero, Danny, who comes home to find his wife Delia and their baby barely existing on his service allotment. It ends with a voice from the audience, "The Man Who Knows," interrupting the action to propose a solution to the problem: the participation of the ordinary American family in the government of society.

The next year, on the recommendation of Herman Shumlin, Miller visited army camps throughout the nation for background material for a screenplay, *The Story of G. I. Joe*, based on Ernie Pyle's collection of human interest stories of military life, *Here Is Your War*. From this trip, he also got material for a book of military reportage, *Situation Normal*, published in 1944. Also in this year, a daughter, Jane, was born to the Millers.

Miller had his first theatrical break late in 1944, with the staging of *The Man Who Had All the Luck* on Broadway.[17] With this play, Miller turned away from social protest and improvement as themes and focused instead on the protagonist's efforts to understand the reasons for his personal success, the "luck" in the play's title. Set in a small farming community in the Midwest, the play looks critically at three incredibly prosperous years in the life of David Frieber. An orphan, David is, in the improbability and sentimentality of his young aloneness, a small parody of the self-made man. What brings him "luck," Miller would persuade us, is what others see in him. He is what they were, what they could have been, what they still might be. After dropping out of school at fourteen, David works at a garage, where a sequence of chance events assures his success as a businessman. But as his prosperity increases and his

ventures diversify, David questions the success he has not earned.
Measuring his own circumstance against that of Amos Beeves,
whose father worked with him relentlessly to train him for big
league baseball pitching but who nonetheless failed, David puts
himself in an untenable business position, repudiating the luck that
has sustained him and affirming his own work and self-worth. Miller regards *The Man Who Had All the Luck* as an inquiry into the
extent to which a man controls his own fate. Convinced of "impending disaster," David tries to bring on that disaster "in order to
survive it and find peace. Instead, he comes to believe in his own
superiority, and in his remarkable ability to succeed."[18]

Unfortunately, Miller himself had no luck with his first Broadway play, which closed in November after a run of only six performances. Though Miller's attitude toward the novel is one of almost
studied disinterest, the play's losses—fifty-five-thousand dollars—
pressured him into writing *Focus*, a study of the destructive power
of anti-Semitism. Set in New York City, the novel follows Lawrence,
a corporation officer with an anti-Semitic bias, through a series of
situations that cause him to be mistaken for a Jew. The cumulative
result of these events is that he moves from being anti-Semitic to
being the object of anti-Semitism. The extent of this shift is demonstrated at the end of the novel when, after a fight with the lone
neighborhood Jew against five young members of the fascist Chris-
tian Front movement, he is unwilling to correct the assumption of
the investigating policeman that he is a Jew.

In 1945, before the end of the war, an event occurred that
reveals some significant notions Miller held concerning the role of
the writer in society and emphasizes the deep commitment he had
made to the fight against anti-Semitism. One evening he turned on
his shortwave set: "and there was a voice which I had never heard
but which spoke perfectly good American advocating the destruction of the Jewish people and justifying the cremation of Jews, and I
was quite astonished because it was such a common American accent, and I waited to the end, and it was being broadcast from Italy,
and it was Ezra Pound."[19]

In December of the same year, when Pound was brought to trial
for treason, Miller attacked him in *New Masses* magazine. In this
article, he refers to the reaction which the Pound case had on the

literary world, especially on those men who defended him in the newspaper *PM* of Sunday, November 25, 1945:

> In a world where humanism must conquer lest humanity be destroyed, literature must nurture the conscience of man. A greater calamity cannot befall the art than that Ezra Pound, the Mussolini mouthpiece, should be welcomed back as an arbiter of American letters . . . [20]

Appearing before the HUAC more than ten years later, Miller explained that he had attacked Pound so virulently not only because it was wartime and Pound was an enemy spokesman but also because Pound's broadcasts threatened him personally.[21]

The bitterness of Miller's reaction to Pound was due not merely to Miller's personal involvement as a Jew but also to Miller's liberal social concern. During the years following World War II, he was still associated with the socialist magazine *New Masses* and was also active in organizations that ranged across the spectrum of the political left. Miller's later descriptions of these times, such as that given before the HUAC, record an indiscriminate affinity for liberal causes that was to be stridently criticized during the politically conservative fifties.

In 1945, Miller also published a radio play, *Grandpa and the Statue*, in which a young soldier, Monaghan, recalls his Irish grandfather's reluctance to contribute to the erection of the Statue of Liberty, until a visit to the statue and a conversation with a soldier dispels his doubts. Though it is too late to offer his dime, he secretly deposits a half-dollar in a pedestal crack.[22]

1947 saw not only the birth of a son, Robert, on May 31, but also the opening of Miller's first successful Broadway play, *All My Sons*, produced by Elia Kazan, at the Coronet Theatre on January 29. Because of the sudden and widespread popularity of *All My Sons*, Miller was now more earnestly sought out by leftist social and political movements to enhance the stature of their specific programs.[23] Political and social issues seemed to draw Miller into their confusion and to evoke from him a statement of belief, an affirmation of his liberal and socialistic principles. In the introduction to *The Story of Gus*, for example, a bit of radio propaganda for the

American wartime merchant marine service, Miller is quoted as
saying:

> No medium of expression can fulfill itself if its forms and its content
> are prescribed beforehand. There is so much you can't say on the radio that
> for a serious writer it presents a blank wall. The answer is freedom, which
> is tightly circumscribed in the present setup. I mean not only freedom of
> speech, but freedom to write a radio play without a format.[24]

Freedom to experiment not only with dramatic form but also with
social issues is the central point of Miller's public statements on the
role of the writer in society. Throughout his career, he emphasizes
the need for continual assertion of the concept of the writer as
interpreter, voice, and conscience of society.

A fitting title for 1949 would be the Year of the Salesman, for
Willy Loman became a national figure from the night of February
10 when *Death of a Salesman* opened at the Morosco Theater.
Miller's most famous play was written in six weeks in his Connecticut home on a typewriter purchased with the money he won for his
first Hopwood award. *Death of a Salesman* won both the New York
Drama Critics' Circle Award and the Pulitzer Prize, the latter given
for the first time that year.

On November 18, 1950, *Death of a Salesman* closed after a
run of 742 performances. Of far more importance for Miller, however, was a meeting he had in that same year with a movie starlet
named Marilyn Monroe. The meeting between Miller and Monroe
took place on the grounds of the Twentieth Century-Fox studios in
California, where she and Cameron Mitchell, a friend of Miller's,
were making a film called *All About Eve*. Miller, with Elia Kazan,
had come west to work on a projected film, entitled *The Hook*,
about labor racketeering on the New York waterfront. According to
Maurice Zolotow, Monroe's biographer, the two saw one another
frequently for several weeks. Monroe was impressed by Miller: she
hung his photograph in her bedroom and, in an interview in
1951, included him among her favorite authors with Tolstoy,
Thomas Wolfe, and Antoine de Saint-Exupery.[25] But Miller's own
public activities for the next few years fail to indicate a reciprocal
attitude.

His political commitments during this time seemed, for the most part, to have limited his literary efforts; his only publication in 1951 was a short story in the March issue of *Harper's*, "Monte Saint Angelo." The story is concerned with Bernstein, a Jew traveling with an Italian companion, Appelo, who visits the ancestral village of his family. While in Appelo's village, Bernstein discovers the nature of his own Jewish heritage in a meeting with an Italian peddler bound for home before sundown on Friday with fresh bread; the peddler ties a bundle like Bernstein's father, yet he has no awareness of the ancient tradition he follows. Bernstein sums up the nature of his Jewish heritage when he says that "the whole history is packing bundles and getting away."[26]

In the growing anti-communist, anti-leftist, and even anti-liberal movements centering on the activities of the House Un-American Activities Committee were the elements that were to break upon Miller for his romance with the left.

On April 10, 1952, Elia Kazan appeared before the HUAC in its investigation of communist infiltration of the motion picture industry and named nine people who were then or who formerly had been members of the Communist Party.[27] In this phase of the committee's operations, many others joined in the hysteria of naming associates not for the sake of informing the HUAC, which in most cases knew the names already, but for the humility value of public confession. Miller, in both *The Crucible* and *After the Fall*, makes this kind of naming procedure a symbol of moral degeneracy and of the breakdown of faith between men.

Miller's literary reaction to the general proceedings of the HUAC and the political tenor of the times was *The Crucible*, which appeared at a time when Miller the writer was to be held responsible for Miller the political leftist. It is important to note, in this regard, that Miller's own definition of the social responsibilities of the writer blurs the distinction between the roles of writer and citizen and quite naturally exposes him to criticism and restrictions on the political plane.

The following year, 1955, marked a transitional time in Miller's life: he was to become deeply embroiled in political conflict; he was to write two plays; and, most importantly, he was to renew his friendship with Marilyn Monroe. At a party of theater people in

May of 1955, after a five-year hiatus, Miller and Monroe met
again. Monroe had been divorced from Joe DiMaggio since October 1954 and was no longer the timid starlet who had been awed by
Miller five years before; Miller was experiencing the deterioration
of his marriage with Mary Grace Slattery, and he had taken to
leading a social life without her.[28]
     There is no evidence from Miller himself to account for the
breakup of his marriage with Mary Grace Slattery; in fact, according to Zolotow, Miller's first wife seems to have been almost ideally
compatible with her husband's interests and temperament. Other
factors, however, may have had some bearing on their separation:
the fact that Mary Slattery was Catholic and the children were
raised without any sense of their Jewish heritage or the fact that her
relationship with Miller's mother was strained.[29] Whatever the
causes of such a complex situation, the results were increasingly and
publicly obvious as Miller and Monroe were together more and
more.
     During this period, Miller's writing activity increased. In June
1955 Combined Artists, a small television firm, asked Miller to
write a script for a New York City Youth Board film. Miller was
enthusiastic about the film and went out with Youth Board workers
for a week in June to see them in action and was moved by their
dedication. For seven weeks in June and July, he spent his mornings
casting for *A View from the Bridge*, his nights with the youth
workers. When, in the middle of August, *A View from the Bridge*
went into the rehearsal stage, he was able to type up an outline of
the film twenty-five pages long to be circulated for backing. Plans
called for the film to be a full-length, professionally-produced
work, with Hollywood stars, to be shown in first-run theaters
throughout the country.
     However, soon after the script outline was finished, reporter
Frederick Woltman attacked Miller in the *New York World-Tele-
gram*, charging him with leftist and communist leanings and demanding, with the editorial backing of his paper, that Miller be
restrained from work on this project. Political action followed, initiated from both federal and local levels, resulting in Miller's being
voted down for the project by the New York City Youth Board. The
reason given by one of the majority members was: "My objection is

he refuses to repent."[30] It is the same kind of objection that condemns John Proctor, the hero of *The Crucible*.

In early 1956, Miller's leftist past was made an issue by conservative and anti-communist elements in government and in the entertainment industry. As a result of this investigation, Miller was subpoenaed to appear before the HUAC in June.[31] In the midst of Miller's political difficulties, he and Monroe surprised the nation by announcing that they had been secretly married in New York in late June of that year. Richard H. Rovere, writing in the *Spectator*, commented that the marriage was "symbolic, portentous, rich in paradoxes and fulfillments. And of course it was, as it should have been, full of good theater. What a backdrop! What timing! What a way to steal a scene."[32]

Miller's appearance before the House Un-American Activities Committee at this time marks the convergence of his political activities and his concepts of society and the writer's role. He answered in an almost conversational manner all questions regarding his own activities in liberal, left-wing, and communist-sponsored organizations, speaking freely and honestly. Regarding his attacks in his plays and in published essays on the HUAC, Miller candidly acknowledged and defended his opposition to the committee.

In Miller's discussion of the Smith Act, which prohibits advocating overthrow of the government by force, he made a point about the dangers of penalizing advocacy and its relation to the writer: "In other words, if advocacy of itself becomes a crime, in my opinion, one can be penalized without overt action, but we are smack in the middle of literature, and I don't see how it can be avoided."[33]

Miller expands on this concept of the writer-artist later on in the proceedings:

The artist is inclined to use certain rights more than other people because of the nature of his work.

Most of us may have an opinion. We sit once or twice a week or we may have a view of life which on a rare occasion we have time to speak of. That is the artist's line of work. That is what he does all day long and, consequently, he is particularly sensitive to its limitations.[34]

When asked by the HUAC to name the writers who were present at communist writers meetings he attended in New York

City, Miller refused. Miller asserted, essentially, the precedence of the individual moral conscience over a law of the society and associated, at least implicitly, his refusal with the right of the writer to take supralegal action where necessary. This belief in the primacy of the individual is a theme that pervades Miller's writings and is seen in its most assertive form in the characters of John Proctor in *The Crucible* and Eddie Carbone in *A View from the Bridge*, who assure their own deaths by breaking the laws of their societies to affirm their personal sense of justice. Miller's refusal to name his associates, although commendable on moral grounds, resulted in his conviction for contempt of Congress on May 31, 1957.

In late 1957, Marilyn Monroe, who had become pregnant in the spring of the year, lost the child. As an act of love for his distraught wife, Miller set himself to writing a screenplay for her. He chose as a basis for his work his short story "The Misfits," scheduled for publication in the October 1957 edition of *Esquire*. In its short story version, "The Misfits" describes the efforts of three men, who capture mustangs for a dog food manufacturer, to resist the inevitable encroachment of an impersonal society. The only two significant characters in the story, the middle-aged Gay Langland and the young Perce Howland, live by the motto that "anything's better'n wages." Roslyn is not seen in the story and functions only to sympathize with the horses. In the screenplay, Miller expands the story in order to focus on the character of Roslyn. The general effect of the screenplay is a feeling that Miller evades issues he treated honestly in the short story by creating a sympathy with Roslyn's tenderness but an inability to reconcile such sympathy with the often cruel realities of the world. In 1958 *The Misfits* was filmed, with Monroe playing Roslyn.

During this time, increased public support for the honesty of Miller's stand before HUAC and the personal justness of his refusal to name names was moving government authorities to reconsider the Miller citation. On August 7, the nine-man court of the United States Court of Appeals for the District of Columbia unanimously reversed his conviction, stating that the HUAC had not given him sufficient warning of the risk of contempt. Following the reversal, Miller found the stigma of HUAC charges fading and literary doors reopening to him.

But Miller's domestic life was in trouble. On January 21, 1961, Monroe applied for a Mexican divorce on grounds of incompatibility of character. It was granted three days later. Miller's mother died in this year as well, at the age of eighty. Miller kept from the public eye for the rest of the year, publishing only two short pieces, "Please Don't Kill Anything," in *Redbook*, and "The Prophecy," in *Esquire*.[35]

"Please Don't Kill Anything" is an emotional vignette in which a husband and wife walking along the beach come upon some fishermen who, in sorting their catch, toss the fish they don't want on the sand to die. The wife's reaction to such a waste of life is much like Roslyn's in *The Misfits*, where Roslyn causes Gay to cut the ropes that bind the mustangs; here she makes her husband throw the discarded fish back into the surf. Both acts merely delay death for the animals, but both acts also evoke a temporary sense of emotional satisfaction. "The Prophecy" seems like a dry run of *After the Fall* in its presentation of near-adultery, subsequent alienation between friends, divorce, and the sensitive witness of it all, Joseph Kersh, who suffers the same kind of feelings that Miller later ascribes to Quentin. A typical sentence reads like notes for every other scene in *After the Fall*. "And treason to others—to Joseph Kersh—was the ultimate destruction, worse even than treason to himself, living with a wife he could not love."[36] This passage also illustrated a quality that later became an obvious flaw in his writing: his use of situations and characters too easily comparable to those in his personal life.

On February 17, 1962, just over a year after his marriage to Monroe was dissolved, he and Ingeborg Morath, a photographer for the French service Magnum, were married in New Milford, Connecticut. In dark contrast to the happiness of his new marriage was the news of Marilyn Monroe's death on August 5, 1962, due—as was Maggie's in *After the Fall*—to an overdose of sleeping pills. During the wave of public grief that followed her death, Miller was silent, avoiding the attendant sensationalism that such a public tragedy generates. The innumerable public recollections of interviewers and acquaintances which followed Marilyn's death must have evoked painful memories. In a posthumously-published interview made before her divorce from Miller, Marilyn had revealed, pathetically and unconsciously, that her marriage to Miller was for her not a union of two stable adults but rather a relationship of a confused child-like woman and a man who represented security.[37] Later in 1962, Miller returned to writing about the problem of juvenile delinquency, receiving far greater public acceptance at this time than he had in 1956. In an article entitled "The Bored and the Violent," which appeared in the November issue of *Harper's*, Miller developed the thesis expressed in the editors' headnote: that the brutality of adolescent gangs in major cities is symptomatic of a worldwide spiritual crisis.[38] Miller's writing in "The Bored and the Violent" is strident and pointed in its emphasis on the writer's concern for bringing about moral improvement in his society. He stresses the spiritual flaws of modern man in an almost evangelical manner.

For the greatest part of a year after the publication of "The Bored and the Violent," Miller virtually withdrew from public notice. The only significant activity of a public nature he pursued was to run for a position on the Library Board of Directors of Roxbury, Connecticut, in October 1963. Miller lost to novelist William Styron and Manfred Lee (co-author of the "Ellery Queen" stories) and to John H. Humphrey, whose parents founded the first library in Roxbury. It is one of the small ironies of his career that Miller, who so forcefully moves his audiences through his plays, should fail to win support in an election strongly based on intellectual and literary qualifications.[39]

He spent most of that year working on a new play, the writing of which had been rumored since 1960. Entitled *After the Fall*, it was to generate more critical controversy than any other play Miller had written. Anticipating criticism of the play as being overly autobiographical, Miller acceded at the time of the reading that all his plays were, but he claimed that this one was less so.[40] The point that Miller fails to emphasize in his replies to his critics is that for him autobiography and fiction are complements. Though compelled to write his *apologia* in dramatic form, Miller refused to admit that some critics would read Quentin and see Arthur Miller.

Almost immediately, *After the Fall* became popularly know as "that play about Marilyn Monroe." Critics with near unanimity deplored the excessive use of autobiographical details. Robert Brustein, writing for the *The New Republic*, represented critical opinion when he termed it "a three-and-one-half-hour breach of taste, a confessional autobiography of embarrassing explicitness."[41] In reply, Miller himself reemphasized the point he had made at the reading of *After the Fall* in October of 1963, strongly denying the obvious autobiographical implications audiences saw in the play.[42]

One of the major themes of *After the Fall*, the insistent concentration on the individual's responsibility for the guilt incurred by his society, was linked with an assignment Miller had for the *New York Herald Tribune* as a special commentator at the Frankfurt Nazi trials in March of 1964. In summarizing his reactions to the meaning of the trials, Miller emphasized the interrelatedness of all men within the context of an evil act.

Miller was to use this concept as the cardinal theme of his second play for the Lincoln Center Repertory, *Incident at Vichy*. The publicity and sensationalism that had surrounded *After the Fall* had produced in Miller a marked sensitivity to criticism, and, in an interview with Barbara Gelb in November 1964, he emphasized that he had no obligation either to explain his play to an audience or to be influenced by criticism, particularly following "the nimbus of myth and hysteria" that greeted *After the Fall*.[43] That this attitude represents an aberrant mood, out of character with his personal and dramatic philosophy, is demonstrated by the fact that Miller wrote a lengthy apologia for *Incident at Vichy*—"Our Guilt for the World's Evil"—which appeared in the January 3, 1965, issue of the *New York Times Magazine*. In the article, Miller takes great care to explain and analyze the theme and personal and social ramifications of the play. He even chides his audiences for their critical errors:

It is not "about Nazism," or a wartime horror tale; they do not understand that the underlying issue concerns us now, and that it has to do with our individual relationships with injustice and violence. But since a few critics persist in their inability to differentiate between a play's story and its theme, it is just as well to make those differences plain.[44]

The reviews of *Incident at Vichy*, which opened on December 3, 1964, were generally unfavorable. Criticism focused upon Mill-

er's didacticism, for the most part agreeing with Robert Brustein's
assessment of the piece as a sermon on responsibility.[45]

Despite the sour reception, however, Miller's works enjoyed
great popularity in the European literary world, and, in the early
months of 1965, the playwright traveled extensively on the Continent to oversee productions of his plays. In May 1965 it was announced that he had been nominated for the presidency of International PEN, an organization whose initials stand for poets,
playwrights, editors, essayists, and novelists.[46] For the following
twelve months, Miller concentrated less on writing than on prom-
ulgating his beliefs about the social and political importance of the
writer. The theme of the thirty-fourth PEN Congress, "The Writer
as Independent Spirit," provided Miller with the occasion to extend
his definition of the writer as social commentator to other cultures
and to record his almost fatalistic vision of the contemporary situation:

It is my hope that P.E.N., in all of the Centers around the world, will
investigate as profoundly as possible the distinctive role and the possibilities
for literature. I think the time is growing short. I think the time is coming
when there will be such a suspicion of the unique invention of an author
that it will be as in Dante's time—a curio—except that the future of literature will be lost.
Poets began literature: we're liable to finish it.[47]

That same year, 1966, Miller's *Death of a Salesman* was televised, with great popular success, to an audience of approximately
seventeen million, twenty times the number who saw the play on
Broadway. In an interview, Miller spoke of his belief in the critical
intelligence of the average viewer, averring that if networks would
commit themselves to creative programming, their executives would
be astonished to discover that quality productions can have wide
appeal.[48]

He gave added emphasis to his belief in and sympathy for the
common man by the publication in 1967 of a collection of short
stories entitled *I Don't Need You Any More*. Although most of the
stories were published previously, the earliest dating to 1951, and
the quality of the stories was uneven, Miller's concern for the ordinary man gave the collection coherence. But the strong, often-cou-

rageous voice of Miller the dramatist was cramped by the more-confining short-story form. Thomas Lask, recognizing Miller's aesthetic discomfort with the unfamiliar genre, commented that the Miller of this collection was neither graceful nor relaxed.[49]

Nor did Miller as political spokesman ever relax. In 1967, when protests against the Vietnam War were crescendoing, Miller characteristically rode the strongest winds. In an article entitled "It Could Happen Here—And Did," published a few days before the CBS presentation of *The Crucible*, he addresses the political relevance of his art. Dismissing critics who saw the play simply as an analogy to McCarthyism, he argues that it is about something of far-wider and deeper significance: "When irrational terror takes to itself the fiat of moral goodness, somebody has to die." The lessons of the play, he claims, have been at least partially learned by people in power; despite protests, Americans "as a whole have not rallied the unwashed to go hunting for people whose bad thoughts are cheating us of victory." Wary of the strength of frustration that builds up in a society during the possibly long years of an unwanted and unwinnable war, he worries aloud about "the slide into darkness," where the serpent of madness lies for the nation, and, in language that evokes the scriptures, says that *The Crucible* was written so "the coiled thing in the public heart might die of light."[50]

This article is one of the clearest and most eloquent of Miller's statements not about the generically prophetic role of the writer but specifically about himself. He reasserts what he had learned during his days in the shadow of Joe McCarthy and the Congressional witch hunters about the need of constant vigilance in the face of social paranoia and governmental brutality.

In 1967, Miller returned to Russia to gather more materials for a book. In this year also, he was re-elected president of PEN International at the thirty-fifth World Congress in Abidjan, Ivory Coast. From this office, he continued to urge the release of writers held throughout the world for political reasons. It was fitting, therefore, that when a writers' manifesto signed by three hundred leading Czech authors and intellectuals deploring oppressions of freedom in their country was published in the *Sunday Times* of London, Miller was among a small group of renowned writers (including Sartre, Steinbeck, and Bertrand Russell) to whom it was addressed.

As if to emphasize the increasingly international stature of both the man and his works, the Philadelphia Lyric Opera staged the American premiere of an operatic version of *The Crucible* by Renzo Rossellini entitled *Uno Sguardo dal Ponte*. Originally produced at Rome in the spring of 1961, the opera had played in Frankfurt, Barcelona, Zagreb, and Cairo. Its critical reception in America was mixed, with praise for the strength of Miller's story but little applause for Rossellini's music.

The fullness of both artistic success and social activism worked as a tonic on Miller. During all his activity on behalf of peace and human rights, his literary work, this time on getting *The Price* into production, moved steadily on. In early December, he was described as "zestful" as he worked on rehearsals of the play at the New Amsterdam Theater just before it left town for a trial run in Philadelphia.[51]

His final public statement of the year was a trenchant article on the op-ed page of the *New York Times*.[52] In it he presents images of American ineptness and unthinking cruelty in the attempts to "save" Vietnamese peasants who wanted none of the alleged protection. Miller writes of the forced removal of peasants from their lands and the destruction of their homes by American soldiers to deny shelter to the Viet Cong. Then he asks the crucial question; he asks why Vietnamese peasants don't burn down their own houses. Miller speaks of the scorched earth policy of peoples of the past who would deny all to the invader, then warns that Vietnam is different. Exploring the ironies of the situation, he claims that there is a new age upon his generation, the Age of Abdication.

In 1968, one of the most turbulent years in recent American history, the dualities of nostalgia and relevance vied for dominance in Miller's life. There was a play that treated the former and a Presidential campaign that dealt with the latter.

The Price, which opened on Broadway in February, received mixed reviews, partially because it focused on a situation and on characters removed from the issues that were confronting the nation. Walter Kerr spoke of the play's "obvious thinness" but also of an "astonishingly droll" new face of Miller's. Clive Barnes described an audience that had been "deeply moved" by "good theater," but it was not "very serious theater."[53] The play, rich in the Miller tradition of transmogrified biography, makes the final and, thus, resolving statement about a family of two brothers, the older of whom sacrifices all or some significant part of his life for a commitment to his family. Inevitably, this sacrifice frees the younger brother to pursue his dreams. The positive resolution of this major theme in *The Price* makes it, uncharacteristically, a comedy in a dual sense. First, if self-acceptance is the basis of happiness, then the play has a happy, although subdued, ending; second, in Gregory Solomon, the used furniture dealer, Miller creates a truly successful "funny" individual. That Solomon is by far Miller's most successful comic character follows from the wider contextual resolution. Regardless of the reservations of the critics, the reaction of the playgoing public was strongly appreciative. As an added mark of the public's appreciation of his work, a month later he was honored by Viking, his publisher, who presented him with a facsimile in gold of the title page of *Death of a Salesman* when sales reached one million copies.

The happiness in his professional life seemed to give Miller an added strength when a nearly overwhelming repetition of devastating shocks struck the nation in 1968. In his reaction to the assassination of Robert Kennedy in June,[54] he moves from the death of the individual man to the society at large to find a reason for such a maddening act. Contending that violence exists because we honor violence daily, he pleads for the end of poverty, for racial justice, and, especially, for an end to the war in Vietnam.

Miller's activity was not limited as it had been so often in the past to writing about injustice or of the need for change. In late June, he entered the arena of party politics successfully and, as a McCarthy delegate, was chosen to attend the state Democratic convention in Hartford. In Hartford, he offered a resolution that the delegates call on the United States government to cease bombing North Vietnam and to work to bring all involved parties to negotiations. The convention did not act on this resolution. Along with five other McCarthy delegates, including actor Paul Newman, he was a member of the Connecticut delegation to the fateful Democratic National Convention held in Mayor Richard Daley's Chicago.[55]

Writing about those confused days of street theater, protests, riots, and police brutality in an article entitled "The Battle of Chica-

go: From the Delegates' Side," Miller offered an artist's, an idealist's, point of view. Concerning the struggle of the McCarthy delegates against the supporters of the Johnson-backed forces, Miller
says, "There were two Americas in Chicago, but there always are.
One is passionately loyal to the present, whatever the present happens to be; the other is in love with what is not yet." For Miller, there
was a violence both inside the convention, "where there was disci-
pline but no leadership," and outside, where no one knew "when
the police and the troops would again go berserk."[56]

He did not stay to see the final session and the approval of
Hubert Humphrey's candidacy because he believed the unseen hand
of President Lyndon Johnson moved the controls. In fact, he joined
in a protest march on the floor of the convention when the plan
supporting the Johnson war effort was adopted. The next morning,
on his Connecticut lawn before the sun rose, he pondered what had
been done. Smug, cynical, brutal Chicago was past, he decided, and
it was his time to move on. The opportunity came in a request from
London to protest the Soviets' jailing of writers in Prague.[57] He
would not only join that activity on behalf of the Czechs but would
raise his voice to protest the ban imposed on Solzhenitsyn's work by
the Soviet Union.

Even such quixotic enterprises with so little chance of being
heeded, let alone acted upon by the Russian invaders of Czechoslovakia, did not deter him from an unyielding commitment to achieving the freedom of the individual. Miller was certainly not alone in
becoming embroiled in the passionate and overridingly important
issues that nearly unhinged American society in 1968. However,
unlike many of his fellow citizens, his protests and his actions to
change the tenor of things in this year were part of a long personal
tradition.[58]

After the intensity of 1968, 1969 was a full but decidedly less
hectic year for Miller. Continuing his commitment to peace, he was
a participant (along with such notables as Norman Cousins and
David Rockefeller) in the Fifth Dartmouth Conference of US and
Soviet Citizens held to explore ways to end the arms race. And,
professionally, his original optimism about the staying power of
The Price was borne out when, after a successful run of 425 perfor-

mances in just over a year, the play closed at New York's 46th Street Theater. It would open in London in March. Although he continued to be active in his support of the freedom of writers to express themselves without fear of political repression, he resigned as president of PEN International at the organization's thirty-sixth congress in France. In his farewell remarks, he stressed the need for young writers to "have the imagination to go out into the highways, byways and ghettos to make it apparent that the writer belongs to the street and not to the power."[59]

Characteristically, he refused to allow the Greek government power to publish *The Price* or any other of his works because it had incarcerated sixteen writers for political reasons. To sanction publication of his plays, he said, "would inevitably give the color of freedom to a regime which actively and cruelly represses it among its own citizens."[60]

Miller also continued his fight against the Johnson Administration's Vietnam policy by joining with Eli Wallach, Robert Ryan, and Gino Giglio, the company manager of *Man of La Mancha*, to make a film version of his short antiwar piece "The Reason Why" on his Connecticut farm.

But it was the Soviet Union that figured largest in Miller's writing and political concerns in 1969. In the same year that he attended the Dartmouth Conference, he published a book highly appreciative of the character of the Russian people and vigorously organized a campaign to criticize that nation's refusal to allow its writers to express themselves freely. As one of his last official acts as PEN International president, Miller, influenced by a series of articles written by Anatoly Kuznetsov, encouraged the Congress to investigate and denounce censorship of Soviet writers. In November, with his wife Inge Morath, he published *In Russia*,[61] based on visits in 1965 and 1967 in which the authors ranged from Moscow to Tashkent. Throughout, there is an obvious and genuine affection for the diverse Soviet peoples (his favorites are the Georgians) that allows Miller to criticize the political system from a position of basic fairness.

Indeed, Miller avoids easy and simplistic comparisons between Russians and Americans and instead points out the complexities of

the act of judgment so that the reader is inclined not toward alienation but rather toward understanding, sympathy, and reconciliation.
Called by the publisher "a studio book," *In Russia* is liberally illustrated with Morath's photographs, which employ contrast as a device to emphasize whatever is asymmetrical, ironic, human, and—
on occasion—humorous.

Less than a month after the publication of *In Russia*, Miller
framed a letter sent to Moscow over the names of a number of
American writers (including, of course, his own) that protested the
expulsion of Aleksandr I. Solzhenitsyn from Russia. With typical
Miller bluntness, it rejected the criminality of an artist's refusal to
accept state censorship and deplored a government's persecution of
an artist when foreigners published his books.[62]

Early in 1970, Miller turned his attention from foreign lands to
his own small Connecticut community. With a group of townspeo-
ple, including his neighbor William Styron, he came to the defense
of Mrs. Clinton Hanover, an English teacher in the local elementary
school who was denounced by some school board members for
refusing to say the Pledge of Allegiance in her classroom. Specifically, she objected to saying the words "with liberty and justice for all"
because she believed it obvious that for too many Americans the
words did not apply. It was as though Mrs. Hanover were playing
out the role of a classical Miller protagonist. Only this time he
could do something more than just delineate the movement toward
an inexorably tragic ending.

In May, Miller was honored by Brandeis University as recipient
of a Creative Arts Award Medal, which cited his "eloquent and
stirring statements."[63] All the while that Miller continued with ad-
mirable consistency and integrity to live out the values for which
Brandeis praised him, the Soviet government was planning another
kind of recognition for him. In November, with typically ursine
vengeance, the Soviet government reacted to Miller's book and,
more importantly, to his support for Solzhenitsyn: all his books
were banned and a television production of *The Price* was canceled.

Miller recorded his reaction in an op-ed piece in the *New York
Times*, noting the presence of shock but the absence of surprise. He
commented ironically on being blacklisted first in his own country
and now in the Soviet Union: "Comrades, shake hands with the

House Committee on Un-American Activities." His assessment, however, avoids self-pity and takes the higher ground:

> This ban is an extreme act. The wind is rising. And the light and breezy edge of it that has brushed my sleeve reminds me again of what a spirit lives in Aleksandr Solzhenitsyn who has pitted his very existence against its force. One can only marvel at such a man. But he is not alone.

Miller sees, rightly, in Solzhenitsyn the living embodiment of a man like his own John Proctor and, in an allusion to *The Crucible*, speaks of the Soviet government disgracing its country, even as the witch-hunters disgraced ours: "The tragedy, evidently, is fated to continue long after its lessons should have been learned."[64]

Miller's admonitory statements about repression, like Jefferson's statement that "the price of liberty is eternal vigilance," are neither paranoid nor foolish if danger does not come alive to prove their validity. In fact, it can be forcefully argued that such wariness is the ultimate in both pragmatism and wisdom. Miller, obviously, does not separate the role of playwright from some private self that desires to burrow away secure from the issues in his works. Unlike many of his fellow citizens, he is compelled to push out beyond the borders of what is comfortable to a place where ordinary courage fails. Then he writes about it because everybody should know. It is for this reason that he seems, for people who refuse to understand, just some articulate person "looking for trouble."

At this time in his career, however, his professional life was not hampered by his political activities. In February of 1971, two of his plays, *A Memory of Two Mondays* and *The Price*, appeared on television. Even though he had referred to television in an article a few years before as a "blanding machine,"[65] the appearance, especially of *The Price*, indicated that there had developed from Miller's point of view at least some spice and marrow in the cultural diet served to the American public. Television critics mixed their judgments in much the same way as their Broadway colleagues had. But two weeks after Julius Novick's comments on Miller's "ponderous self-seriousness" appeared, the *New York Times* published a group of letters from viewers—all pro-Miller.[66]

The revival of Miller's adaptation of Ibsen's *An Enemy of the*

People at The Vivian Beaumont Theater in Lincoln Center in March was praised by Clive Barnes as one of Miller's best plays and panned by Kerr as melodramatic.[67] The public verdict expressed at the box office was in Miller's favor.

In the spring, Miller was instrumental in rousing support for the Brazilian playwright Augusto Boal of São Paolo's Arena Theater, who was arrested for his presentation of avant-garde "newspaper theater" satirizing government policies. Boal arranged and set to music official reports, news releases, and editorials in such a way that the ironies, contradictions, and deceptions of the government were presented in its own words. Because of international protests on Boal's behalf, the playwright was freed from imprisonment; he then journeyed to New York under Miller's sponsorship to introduce his work to the American public.

Professionally, the rest of the year was largely taken up with preparing *The Creation of the World and Other Business* for Broadway with producer Robert Whitehead, director Harold Clurman, and cast. It would be, Miller told a reporter with unfortunately prophetic accuracy, " a catastrophic comedy."[68]

In early December, he was elected to membership in the American Academy of Arts and Letters, along with Eudora Welty, Barbara Tuchman, Isabel Bishop, Isamu Noguchi, and Saul Bellow. Honors of this sort were coming more and more for Miller despite, or perhaps because of, his ingrained tendency to question authority. By now, it was a trait that was familiar and, thus, unthreatening to a society that had seen recent evidence of protest that made anything Miller had done seem tame.

Then, in 1972, a curious element emerges in Miller's writing, a warm comic urge embodied in *The Creation of the World and Other Business.* But it is not accompanied by a slacking off in political activities or in speaking out for his beliefs. That same year, he attacked the three-year sentence imposed on Ralph Ginzburg after a 1963 obscenity conviction was upheld after a nine-year battle by a five-to-four Supreme Court vote. He protested the barring of four Cuban film directors from visiting the US. He condemned the dismissal of the Jewish dancer Valery Panov from the Kirov State Dance Theater of Leningrad simply for asking permission to emigrate. And, on the weekend before the presidential election, he became strongly critical of his fellow Americans for wanting "the theatrical impression of a man successfully impersonating integrity," namely Richard Nixon, in the White House.[69]

Professionally, Miller continued to work for the greater vitality of drama and its availability to a wider public. He gave, for example, permission to produce *Death of a Salesman* with an all-black cast in Baltimore in April, attending the performance personally and applauding. In the same month that a revival of *The Crucible* opened at the Vivian Beaumont, he published an article in the *New York Times* entitled "Arthur Miller vs. Lincoln Center." In it he attacked the center's board of directors claiming it never intended to establish a repertory theater; because of a similar mentality that pervaded America, he charged, we are on our way to becoming a second-class cultural power.[70]

He also reviewed the book *In Hiding* by Ronald Fraser about Manuel Cortes, a Spanish socialist condemned to death under the Franco regime who had hidden in his own house for thirty years until a general amnesty was granted. His remarks reveal his own affinity with the courageous and unyielding Cortes: the book left him not in despair but in awe, feeling that he had been given a truth that, like Manuel's spirit, will not die.[71]

All this is familiar Miller territory. However, to understand the background for the shift in perspective that moved him to try his hand at comedy, it is helpful to consider two interviews he had in that year: one with Tom Buckley, the other with Josh Greenfield. In the combination, he speaks more candidly and warmly than he had since an interview with Robert Sylvester in 1949.

He tells Buckley that he had begun *The Creation of the World and Other Business* in 1970, for his own enjoyment, but when it began to invent itself, he decided to pursue it seriously. Nonetheless, he thoroughly enjoyed writing the play over the next six weeks. When asked why he had sought out the Scriptures as a source of dramatic inspiration, Miller replied that in his study he had "a handful of books, . . . and one of them has always been the Bible. I read it, the Old Testament usually, because the new one I can't understand too easily, so I've always had a rather intimate feeling about it."[72]

Much of the reason for his shift to comedy is associated with

Miller's fascination with the book of Genesis. He is drawn to the spiritual reassurance of a story so fixed in our culture by innumerable repetitions that it has the comfort, if not of scientific fact, at least of mythic validity. In the Greenfield interview, Miller describes himself as moving away from naturalism toward symbolism and the mythological.[73]

Most importantly—and Buckley's emphatic placement of this fact in the last paragraphs of the article is significant—in August, Miller's son made him a grandfather for the first time. It was, thus, with more than coincidence that Miller moved from this play to a statement about the play as an affirmation of youth and life, as an added explanation for a recent development in his writing:

My experience with this play is that the younger you are the more it will move you. . . . The world of this play is the world of the young. It isn't a world in which an old, creaky philosopher is making his peace. This is the world of creation, not of burial.[74]

In the Greenfield interview, the amity between the two Brooklyn boys is enhanced by the relaxed afternoon at Miller's Roxbury home. The result is a piece that presents a rarely-seen human side of the playwright. We learn, for instance, that he is given to eating Mallomars, drives a Mercedes 280 SEL and an old Volkswagen, starts reading a lot of novels but finishes few, is an accomplished woodworker, and, when he writes in the cabin he built out on a rise of his property, he urinates out the door instead of trekking back to the house.

In both interviews, when Miller speaks of his own literary reputation and of the essential role that drama plays in every culture, there is a reflective and philosophical tone to his words. By 1972, it was clear that Miller—raised in Harlem and Brooklyn, a product of the Depression and World War II—was not merely a survivor but a success. Like Ben Loman, who emerged from the jungle with a fortune, Miller escaped the chaos of New York City to live on 350 acres of Connecticut farmland that his playwriting earned for him. Moreover, Miller could live beyond and without Broadway, which, he felt, could no longer support the kind of theater of affirmation in which he believes.[75]

All these good feelings about himself would help insulate him from the harsh and abrupt fate that would soon overtake a most spiritually personal play.[76] In November, after production problems with *The Creation of the World and Other Business* that saw Clurman and starring actors Hal Holbrook and Barbara Harris leave the show less than a month before it opened, it was obvious that there was trouble in Miller's paradise. When the play opened at the Schubert Theater on November 30, the results were, to use a word Miller had whimsically chosen in happier times, "catastrophic." Barnes, an undaunted Miller admirer, called the play "a victory of craft over artistry and of mind over matter." Kerr, in a not-surprising negative comment, remarked that "the evening ends with a harangue and a whimper."[77] On December 16, after only twenty performances, *The Creation of the World and Other Business* closed. It was the worst experience a Miller play had had since *The Man Who Had All the Luck* closed after six performances in 1944.

Although he would later prove not to have given up the idea of dramatizing the Book of Genesis, in 1973 he went virtually on retreat from Broadway. He received an appointment to his alma mater, the University of Michigan, as an adjunct professor in residence. Most of his professional time at Michigan was spent working with the University Players on scenes from *The American Clock*, on which Miller had been working since the spring of 1970. He also found his international audience to be appreciative and profitable. NBC announced that it would include some Miller plays in a trade package deal it had made with the BBC.

In addition, as if to emphasize his separation from Broadway, in November Miller broke a twenty-five-year-old policy of refusing permission for performances of *Death of a Salesman* within one hundred miles of New York. He allowed the Philadelphia Drama Guild to revive the play for three weeks in February of 1974.

Instinctively opposed to the suppression of writers who raised their voices in political dissent, Miller and others petitioned the United Nations Secretary General Kurt Waldheim to declare 1974 "World Amnesty Year." In midyear he turned his aim on the White House and condemned President Nixon's unwillingness to protest Soviet persecution of dissidents when he met with Premier Leonid I.

Brezhnev: Nixon's silence, he contended, sent the message that the United States was a "moral nullity."[78]

Yet even as he waged the battle for freedom and integrity, Miller returned to the symbolism of the Book of Genesis in search of both insight and happiness. Most of his professional concerns in this year were with *Up from Paradise*, the musical version of *The Creation of the World and Other Business*, or with the television production of *After the Fall*.

In describing his dramatic experimentation with the musical at Michigan, he uses the words "joyful" and "playfulness." In contrast, he speaks somberly of the 1972 Broadway version that failed, he claimed, because it was heavy and psychologically overdone. He now spoke of achieving what he was aiming at originally, "a metaphor for the ingestion of God by man. Adam destroys God on stage and one second later resurrects him in his memory. Adam is God on earth."[79] Miller's unorthodox theology aside, he does speak with a firm, if paradoxical, belief in his revisions.

Perhaps it was the energy of the student actors or being back in a place where the road to success began that made the difference. Whatever the reason, Miller spoke in a decidedly unaccustomed voice. He sounded as if he was having fun being away at college. He spoke of the possibility of a university tour with the play and even of an off-Broadway production. Then he added a wry comment that spoke significantly of his attitude toward the New York Theater Establishment: he didn't have to prove anything on Broadway.[80]

After NBC produced a two-and-one-half hour presentation of *After the Fall* in December, Miller found himself once again the target of heavy attack from a number of critics who couldn't get past the autobiographical suggestions of the play. Many agreed in spirit with John J. O'Connor who, despite seeing it as "sincere soul-searching by a man of intelligence," nevertheless judged it finally "an egotistical abomination" that is "inflated out of all proportion to the almost banal reality."[81] It is no wonder that Miller found increasing happiness, at least for a while, in being far away from Broadway and the *New York Times*.

In 1975, he brought *Death of a Salesman* back to New York, but, predictably, off-Broadway at the Circle in the Square. The production, this time starring George C. Scott, won inevitable high praise.

In a reflective interview concerning *Salesman's* return, Miller takes the long view both of the play and of Broadway. Setting the tone as elder statesman of the American theater, he remarks, half seriously, that in the years since the play's debut he was "twenty-five years older and a year and a half wiser." In assessing the state of contemporary theater, he saw a certain lassitude and passivity. It was "reflecting, rather than originating. There grew a sense of no longer being open to life, but of being scared by it." Touching *Salesman's* enduring universality, he notes, "No country—either Communist or Fascist—has banned it" and adds that in America it ran into trouble only in Chicago where the American Legion once picketed it because of his anti-McCarthy views.[82]

In other areas, expectedly, he spoke out for the rights of oppressed writers: for those harassed and imprisoned by the government of the state of Iran and for Czechs whose "spring" of literary freedom in 1967 he contrasts with the present "winter" when people who can bring light to darkness are in prisons.[83] He also appeared as part of a panel of literary people before the Senate Permanent Subcommittee on Investigation to prod the government to work for the freedom of writers worldwide. Bluntly summing up his point of view, Miller said that the United States, historically, does not care.[84]

Typically, Miller showed his untiring dedication to setting things right, in his writing, in his country, and in the world. Finally, there was in this year a most intriguing and dramatic manifestation of Miller's compulsion to see justice done.

He took up the case of Peter Reilly, of Canaan, Connecticut, a young man who was accused and convicted of savagely murdering his mother, Barbara Gibbons, but whom Miller and others believed to have been railroaded by police. Unlike Truman Capote, who wrote *In Cold Blood*, Miller was less interested in writing a story than in overturning injustice. Although he did not use the crime as the basis of one of his own literary productions, he did explain his interest within a literary context. In speaking of the brutality of the murder, Miller cites *Crime and Punishment*, identifying the common element in the two crimes as "Rage, the heart of the

darkness . . ."[85] Too much of what Miller had come to know of
Reilly convinced him that the young man was incapable of such rage
and thus innocent of the murder.

As a result of his concern, Miller asked the *New York Times* to
investigate the conviction. The paper assigned John Corry to do a
series of articles based in part on Miller's study of the case. Working
with James Conway, a former New York City policeman and private
investigator, Miller consulted with detectives of Harlem's Sixth
Homicide Zone, who gave him advice and encouragement. He also
arranged for a new polygraph expert to enter the case. With untiring energy and thoroughness, Miller spent weeks pursuing the
hidden facts of the crime. Throughout, he was sure that the original
conviction wasn't right. With a hint of Humphrey Bogart in his
voice, the playwright-detective explained that he worked so dili-
gently on Peter Reilly's behalf because he knew that had he tried to
write Peter as murderer into a play, an actor would not know how to
play him.[86]

The efforts of Miller and others on behalf of Reilly resulted in a
petition for a retrial on the basis of new evidence. After a process
drawn out over the next ten months, the charges against Reilly were
dropped in light of evidence which was found to have been suppressed by the prosecution in the original trial. Miller was obviously
gratified by the decision, but he characteristically refused to settle
for half-justice: he still wanted to know who killed Barbara Gibbons.[87]

The remainder of the year was, in terms of Miller's usual activity, relatively quiet. In the spring he finished writing *The Archbishop's Ceiling*, and *The Crucible* was produced at Stratford, Connecticut, in June. Once again, the diametrically opposed critical duo of
Barnes and Kerr reviewed the play for the *New York Times*. In the
light of Miller's successful efforts in the Reilly case, Barnes's comments about Proctor were aptly applied to the man who created
him: he has "a moral probity, a social fearlessness, and a conscience
for humanity."[88]

What drives Miller with such persistent fervor derives in large
part from his roots in Judaism. Speaking at a conference on modern
Jewish artists and writers, Miller revealed his own sense of the life
and death urgency of his vocation: "It has to do with the Apoca-

lypse . . . all these people to a profound degree are dancing on the edge of a precipice."[89] In his life, in his work, he comes back, like an Old Testament prophet, to one major chord: the pursuit of moral justice in an erratic and evil-charged world. His only safeguards against moral destruction are his courage and his pen.

Increasingly, Miller is sought out by captive and oppressed writers from around the world who are drawn to his unassailable defense of individual freedom. In 1977, the Czech playwright Pavel Kohout, in an interview with a western journalist, appealed for help. After detailing his sufferings, he said simply, "Tell Arthur Miller. He knows what things are like here."[90] His words were both an act of faith and an affirmation of a moral bond.

Miller responded by organizing more than fifty other literary figures to protest the jailing of Kohout and other Czech writers. As expected, Czech officials ignored the protests. Critics of Miller's seemingly endless capacity for protest saw the reaction of the Czech government as proof of the ineffectiveness of such a quixotic approach that was futile at worst, self-serving at best.

In the spring, *The Archbishop's Ceiling*, his first major play since 1972, opened at the Kennedy Center's Eisenhower Theatre in Washington, DC. Miller described it as "a dramatic meditation on the impact of the immense state power upon human identity and the common concept of what is real and illusory in a small European capital today."[91]

Miller considered bringing the play to New York after its projected three-week run. However, critical reaction was overwhelmingly negative. In referring to the main premise of the play, which deals with the secret taping of a dissident's conversations, Richard L. Coe made a representative judgment: "The subject of bugging is as fatal to Arthur Miller's play as it was to Richard Nixon's White House."[92]

The intensity of Miller's involvement in a world of moral struggles is balanced by an equally strong need for solitude. Since buying his first house in Connecticut in 1941, Miller has habitually retreated to the land as a source of spiritual restoration. His affinity for gardening and for carpentry encourages a patience that strengthens the spirit. Just beneath the skin of the Brooklyn boy, there is an abiding, perhaps utopian, urge for the simple life.

In *In the Country*, a studio book with photographs by Inge
Morath published in this year, Miller details his affection for the
land and the people who know it well. It is an eclectic, eccentric,
warm view of that part of Connecticut around the Miller hometown
of Roxbury. The heart of the book is expressed in Miller's belief
that "fundamental myths derive from country and village life, particularly the idea of each individual being somehow present in the
leadership of government, personally represented, in effect."[93] A mix
of Jeffersonian agrarianism and Scripture, the book wanders among
wry and affectionate portraits of people and the places they make
their homes.

   Miller's lifework, that combination of his philosophy, actions,
and writings, is based on an elemental concept of humanity. Thus,
the laws that work on Miller's plays originated when the first person recognized his own individuality in relation to another's. Some
might call that a philosophy of Reaction; more accurately, when
applied to Miller, it is one of Responsibility.

   The tensional forces at work in Miller's writings are also classic
examples of the inherently American conflict Walt Whitman speaks
of in the first lines of *Leaves of Grass*: "One's self, I sing, a simple
separate person, / Yet utter the word Democratic, the word En-
Masse." That tension between self and other surfaces in Miller's
comments about the television production of *Fame* in 1978. He
speaks about the obvious overcommercialization of the medium
and then makes a remark that seems so out of character from the
playwright of the ordinary man. One of the difficulties, he says, is
that "on television one faces the great unwashed." The obvious
condescension is intended only to bring the reader up short, since
Miller goes on to call for a theater that will include and engage the
"unwashed." The problem with the contemporary theater is "whether the playwright possesses an artistry broad and deep enough to
engage the understanding and the humanity of so immense an audience." Television, in his judgment, will reach its potential only by
the absolute freedom from censorship.[94]

   With characteristic boldness (some would say simplicity), Miller hurdles over any discussion of degrees of censorship; he says,
simply, "none." In contrast with other "acceptable" activities this

year, such as a protest at the Soviet US Mission, Miller's proposal had to be ignored. To take it seriously would have been too unsettling to people who want to resist and curtail serious and culturally influential drama. *Fame* received lukewarm reviews. O'Connor, for example, called it "a rather insubstantial hour" and added, "The medium alone cannot fatten anemic messages."[95] It is surprising that in criticizing the play O'Connor accepts the basic health of the medium and in no way comments on Miller's article in the same paper just four days before.

In the same month that *Fame* was on NBC, he and his wife set out to the People's Republic of China to gather material for another book. In 1979, upon his return, Miller brought *The Price* back to New York after a trial run at the Spoleto USA Festival in Charleston, South Carolina. The times and the critics had changed in Miller's favor, and the production moved with general applause from the new Harold Clurman Theater to the Playhouse.

Miller's continuing support of artistic freedom through protesting the suppression of Soviet writers and marching on the Czech mission in New York were by this time so expected that only failure to protest would have been noticed. However, the television of Fania Fenelon's *Playing for Time* involved Miller in an impassioned battle with many of his fellow Jews and liberals over an artist's freedom of expression. He wrote the television script for the show, which was based on Fenelon's experiences as a prisoner and conductor of a woman's orchestra in a Nazi death camp. Through a series of events in which Miller was not involved, Vanessa Redgrave, a supporter of the political aims of the Palestine Liberation Organisation (PLO), an anti-Zionist political and paramilitary group, was cast in the leading role. Fenelon, already dissatisfied with Miller's script,[96] was joined by a large and vocal segment of the American Jewish community that was outraged by the affair.

Miller, nevertheless, defended the choice of Redgrave and attacked the critics from California, whom he symbolized as representatives of comfort engaged in "the battle of the Golan Heights being waged in Beverly Hills and a safer place you can't find." He went on to draw parallels with his own career and saw the Redgrave situation to be "as political as when I was blacklisted." Finally, he hammered out the best defense any writer has against a priori censorship: "Just watch the show."[97]

In the middle of the arguments about *Playing for Time*, a film, *Arthur Miller on Home Ground*, by Janet Maslin and Harry Rasky, appeared for a short run at the Carnegie Hall Cinema. Ironically, in contrast to the stormy life of its subject at the time, the film was described as "the work of a good listener."[98] It was more of a comment to be said about a middle-level accountant than about America's most controversial playwright.

In March of 1980, nearly two years after Miller's visit to China, Cao Yu, that country's most respected playwright, came to New York. Both men presented a culture-bridging dialogue at Columbia University entitled "Theater in Modern China." Cao, who had not heard of Miller until 1968, is the author of many tragedies, among which are two plays, *Sunrise* and *Thunderstorm*, which Miller called "impressive, fascinating tragedies of Shanghai life in the decaying China of 40 years ago."[99]

The meeting hall was crowded for the two playwrights' commentary on the nature of drama and the relationship between Eastern and Western forms. The success of the interchange at Columbia was due largely to the compatibility of the writers. As the *New York Times* explained it, "Both have battle scars as dissidents, as thinkers who were menaced by their Governments and who have persisted and overcome."[100]

Later in the year, Miller continued his tradition of political protest when, in a move that disturbed many pro-Israel American Jews, he attacked the expansion of Israeli settlements on the West Bank under the Begin government. More predictably, he wrote to the *New York Times* in support of Solidarity, the workers movement in Poland.

Consistently and primarily, however, Miller worked at his playwriting. *The American Clock* opened at Charleston's Spoleto Festival in the spring, and, despite some rough edges, it was praised by critics. Frank Rich, for example, said that the play was flawed but nearly great and that Miller was now "back in touch with his best subject, the failure of the American dream, and back on top of his talent."[101] At the heart of the play is the Baum family, a pared-down version of Miller's boyhood family: Moe, a businessman broken by the Depression; Rose, his cultured and complaining wife; Lee, their fourteen-year-old son and an aspiring writer. Miller recalls how he based the play initially on *Hard Times*, the Studs Terkel book of interviews about the Depression, but then he says, "I soon realized that my own life was moving into it, until there was very little of Terkel left."[102]

Admitting any autobiographical elements into his plays had become anathema to Miller since *After the Fall*, but, here, the playwright emphasized the connections. He even cast his sister, actress Joan Copeland, as the mother.[103]

After Spoleto, Miller took several months to revise *The American Clock*. During that time, in September, *Playing for Time* was shown on CBS with Vanessa Redgrave in the leading role. Critical reaction to the production was high. O'Connor, often a severe Miller critic in the past, said it was "the best script Mr. Miller has written in years" and praised Redgrave for giving "the most extraordinary performance of her illustrious career."[104]

Two months later, when *The American Clock* opened on Broadway, it received a chilling reaction. Kerr said of the heart of the play, "the Baum family has no story"; Rich reluctantly said of the revised play that it was "smashed almost beyond recognition" because Miller had "tinkered . . . to the point of dismantling it."[105]

In 1981, Miller's Edenic urge surfaced again when he brought out a concert version of *Up from Paradise*, set to music by Stanley Silverman, at New York's Whitney Museum. Miller spoke with confidence of the new version. "Honed down into more of a family structure" in which "God shows more of a parental relationship,"[106] the revised work moved away from the symbolic and somewhat experimental and set him back on solid ground.

Later in the year, in a teasingly unfulfilled item, the *New York Times* suggested that Miller was among those predicted to win a Nobel Prize. The "failure" to win, however, wasn't as significant as the association, for the first time in a semi-official way, of Miller's name with the world's highest mark of literary acclaim.

Fame, even that which hints at the symbols of literary immortality, often comes attended by the anxieties that plague the less accomplished. Twice in 1982 Miller joined with other writers to protect his income: once from the tax collector, another time from a lawsuit that threatened to curtail earnings from his plays.

In the first case, Miller and seventeen other Connecticut writers, including William Styron and Harrison E. Salisbury, protested a change in the state tax code that levied an unincorporated business tax, for the first time in state history, on writers and artists. After a successful lobbying campaign, writers, playwrights, and certain artists were exempted from the tax.

In the second, and decidedly more bitter conflict, the League of New York Theaters and Producers filed an antitrust suit against the Dramatists' Guild. Specifically, the suit attacked the arrangement whereby the author of a play was to receive 5 percent of the first five-thousand dollars of the weekly gross receipts, seven-and-one-half percent of the next two-thousand dollars, and 10 percent of all receipts beyond $7,500. Miller termed the move union busting, and an anonymous "prominent producer" stated that it was directed against the playwrights because they were an "unprotected group."[107] An unwilling Joseph Papp, who was drawn into the suit only because he was a member of the league, spoke out for the writers, calling the suit "an ungentlemanly gesture on the part of people who depend for their living on writers. Writers are the key to the theater; theater can't exist without writers."[108]

The conflict between the two groups was especially ill-timed, coming when the whole of Broadway was threatened by destruction of theaters by real-estate interests to make way for large, high-profit residential/office buildings. Even as he was involved in the antitrust suit, he fought unsuccessfully for the lives of two famous theaters, the Helen Hayes and the Morosco, which were demolished to allow construction of a fifty-story, two thousand-room hotel.

Miller's primary energies that year, however, were directed toward plays rather than protests. In October, *After the Fall* opened at New York's Jewish Repertory Theater, and two new one-act plays, *Elegy for a Lady* and *Some Kind of Love Story*, were produced at the Long Wharf Theater in New Haven. Miller chose to direct both *Elegy*, about a man trying to understand his relationship to a woman he thinks is dying, and its companion piece, essentially a crime story, because, he says, he was not optimistic about explaining them to a director.[109] Unfortunately for Miller, the critical reaction was negative. Rich reviewed the Connecticut productions for the *New York Times*, dismissing the double bill as "a worthy, though unsuccessful, experiment in esthetic by a writer who's prone to thinking big."[110]

If 1982 ended on an unsatisfactory note, the next year provided Miller with a dual triumph: *A View from the Bridge* conquered Broadway and *Death of a Salesman* sold out in Beijing.

Arvin Brown's production of the former in February, in its two-act form, was impressive enough for one critic to claim that the play revived Broadway. Praising the drama, Rich commented that it was "thrilling to watch two long-estranged friends come to one another's rescue in their hour of darkest need." With comfortable and consistent sourness, Kerr panned the production, complaining that "Miller seems as obsessed with his play . . . as the play's longshoreman hero, Eddie Carbone, is obsessed with desire for the niece."[111] But the revival (actually the first Broadway mounting of the two-act version) re-established Miller on Broadway, lending legitimacy to the prospect of subsequent revivals and to the return of America's all-time favorite salesman.

In March, Miller and his wife went to Beijing to produce his most famous play. While the Chinese cast and directors were eager and appreciative, it took Miller some time to give them a sense of the play's social and historical context. In *"Salesman" in Beijing*, a production journal published by Viking in 1984, he gives more of a backstage view of the Chinese *Salesman* than of any other of his plays. The combination of Miller's coaching, a good translation, and a good cast was a success. The Chinese audience wept, cheered, and gave him a standing ovation, affirming the fundamental similarities of human aspiration in two seemingly antipodal cultures. Miller explained the empathetic response: "The Chinese took it as a metaphor for people having to create a persona for society. And the Chinese have always been doing that."[112]

While he was on his Chinese visit, Miller also pushed government officials for a revision of Chinese law to recognize international standards regarding copyrights. Without any protection for the author, Miller pointed out, books could be "legally" pirated in a nation containing one-third of all people on earth.

Later that year, after his return to the States—where, in his absence, fire had struck his home and done seventy-five-thousand dollars in damages — Miller brought the musical *Up from Paradise* to the stage of the Jewish Repertory Theater for a four-week run. It was received as pleasantly entertaining work, or, as Rich termed it, "a casual, warm-spirited and innocuous musical chalk talk."[113]

Even as *Up from Paradise* faded from attention, Miller was involved in more notable work. He was caught in the surge of preparation and publicity for *Death of a Salesman's* return to Broadway in which Dustin Hoffman, whom Jack Kroll called a "skinny little sucked-out shell of a man," would challenge the "rumpled hulk" of the incomparable Lee J. Cobb as Willy Loman.[114] One person who would not appear on stage would be Watergate conspirator G. Gordon Liddy, who had read for the part of Ben Loman but who had not been cast. If Liddy had gotten the part, the imaginative possibilities of Miller's defending him from the attacks of the liberal community would probably have far outdone the Redgrave episode.

At this time, also, Miller was selected to be honored with a handful of other American literary figures by New York University with the prestigious Bobst Medal and was awarded two-thousand-five-hundred dollars.

From the moment the revival of *Death of a Salesman* opened in March 1984, it was an extraordinary success both critically and financially. In the first week of April, it sold 10,322 tickets, grossing more than three-hundred-thousand dollars. Eileen Blumenthal of the *Village Voice* noted that "The substantial power of Miller's play does not come merely from melodramatic manipulation of emotions, but from the deep compassion at its center — and from some fine playcraft." Douglas Watt of the *Daily News* was pleased to report that "the power and compassion of Miller's masterpiece are still capable of moving us deeply." And Benedict Nightingale of the *New York Times* endorsed Willy Loman as "a protagonist who will continue to move and fascinate audiences as long as American drama exists."[115]

Two developments, however, later conspired to sour that success. The first was Dustin Hoffman's insistence that because of the physical demands of the role, the number of weekly performances be reduced from eight to seven. (Helen Hayes, when informed of Hoffman's position, asked, "Have people gotten weaker?")[116] This led to disagreements among the three principal backers: Miller, Hoffman, and producer Robert Whitehead. Whitehead's subsequent withdrawal ended an association with Miller that had begun in 1955 with *A View from the Bridge* and continued through *Incident at Vichy* (1964), *The Price* (1968), *The Creation of the World and Other Business* (1972), and *The Archbishop's Ceiling* (1977).

Miller's second disappointment was that none of the actors in *Salesman* was nominated for a Tony Award. Miller indicated that he was dismayed but not surprised, adding that the excellent reviews the play received must have irked his longtime critics.[117]

But as it so often happens with Miller, when he is subjected to criticism on one hand, high honors come at the other. In August he was announced as one of five artists (the others were Danny Kaye, Gian Carlo Menotti, Lena Horne, and Isaac Stern) who would receive Kennedy Center Art Awards in December.

And at the end of the year, as he was preparing for the ceremonies in Washington, he was also embroiled in a battle over unauthorized use of his work. The Wooster Group, an experimental off-off-Broadway company, was using scenes from *The Crucible* in a work entitled *L.S.D.*, described as "a work that examines the themes of possession, psychedelic drugs and political repression."[118] Despite modifications and attempts to negotiate with Miller, the group came under threat of legal action and cut all references to Miller's play from their production. Miller's comments were, simply, "I don't want to harm them. They were well-intentioned. It was just badly handled."[119]

In 1985–86, Miller made the news on several counts, each predictable for a man whose career has been inseparable from social and political causes. In March 1985, he contributed fifty-thousand dollars to the Hopwood Visiting Writers Fund, established to assure a program of readings and workshops by visiting artists. Later that month, he traveled to Turkey with British playwright Harold Pinter. Acting on behalf of PEN, the two held news conferences in Istanbul on human rights, lending moral support to Turkish writers. In October 1985, he and Alice Walker read from their work at PEN Celebration. Later that month, he and several other writers sided with the Center for Constitutional Rights and the American Civil Liberties Union in challenging the 1952 McCarren-Walter Act, under which Mexican writer Margaret J. Randall was denied permanent residence in the United States.

Domestically, Miller joined six-hundred others who objected in 1985 to architectural plans that would augment the Whitney Museum of Art, presumably corrupting the present building's integrity. And in 1986, a quiet year publicly, he, Dustin Hoffman, Rex Reed, and others in Roxbury, Connecticut, protested a gas company's plan to lay a natural gas line through their properties.

Meanwhile, Broadway revived *The Price*, Trinity Repertory Company *The Crucible*; the Long Wharf Theatre staged *All My Sons*, which was later televised; the London stage revived *The American Clock* and *The Archbishop's Ceiling*, and Lincoln Center hosted Miller's two new one-act plays—all on the heels of what can only be called a national event: in October 1985, the Dustin Hoffman production of *Death of a Salesman* graced the television screens of millions of Americans for whom Willy Loman had become a household word.

And so it goes with Arthur Miller: an unending round of success and failure, harsh reviews and high honors mixed constantly with commitment to the freedom of the individual. When *The Price* was revived in Philadelphia that year, Miller spoke about the focus of the play, and, by obvious and appropriate extension, of the focus of his lifework: the individual. He is fascinated "by the endless possibilities in him for good and evil, by his unpredictability, by the possibilities he has for any betrayal, any cruelty, as well as any altruism, any sacrifice."[120] His attitude toward the individual is one of creative frustration, of wanting to right one more wrong, to create one more play.

In 1985, Miller announced that he would soon begin writing his autobiography. As subject of the book, he sees himself as

a person who has never known how to take a vacation, so all life is either work or a preparation for it. To be fruitful is to be happy. You don't have to feel you've got the tiger by the tail; it's when you can't find the tiger that agony begins.[121]

For Miller, there will always be a tiger burning brightly in the moral darkness.

2

❖❖❖❖❖❖❖❖❖❖❖❖❖❖❖❖❖❖❖❖❖❖❖❖❖❖❖❖❖❖❖❖❖❖❖❖❖

All My Sons

All My Sons opened at Broadway's Coronet Theater on January 29, 1947, in a production directed by Elia Kazan and starring Ed Begley, Beth Merrill, and Arthur Kennedy. It played to an audience that, four years earlier, read the news account of the Truman Committee's investigation into allegedly faulty airplane parts manufactured in Ohio[1] and that was particularly responsive to the question of wartime responsibility, only recently having participated in its country's "return to normalcy." Not surprisingly, the play was an immediate success, running for some 328 performances, winning the New York Drama Critics' Circle Award, and establishing the thirty-two-year-old Miller as among the most promising of America's playwrights.

In *All My Sons*, Joe Keller, owner of a plant manufacturing wartime airplane cylinders for the military, has resumed his comfortable, middle-class life in a middle-American town following a brief prison term. Some three years earlier, the plant had gone into full-scale production to fill a government order. On a day when Keller was late getting to work, his partner, Steve Deever, discovered hairline cracks in the cylinders; Keller, claiming illness, ordered him, by phone, to conceal them. The plant shipped off the cylinders, but the faulty equipment caused several military planes to crash, killing their young pilots. Apparently without conscience, Keller reneged on his promise to Deever to accept responsibility, perjured himself, and allowed his partner to take principal blame.

Keller lives now with his wife and younger son, Chris, all of whom are haunted by the disappearance of Larry, the older son who was a pilot in the war and who was reported missing in action three and one-half years earlier. Keller's wife, Kate, in particular, waits for

Larry's homecoming, unable to accept his death because she connects that death with her husband's guilt. Larry, it turns out, is indeed dead, having committed suicide in a kamikaze flight when he read the accounts of his father's firm's culpability. On the day of his death, he sent his girlfriend, Annie, a letter explaining his shame and his plan, a letter she concealed until now when, hoping to free the family from the ghost of Larry and free Chris from the lingering guilt that threatens their impending marriage, she shows it to the Kellers. The letter precipitates Keller's confession and his decision to shoot himself in a gesture of self-abasement and atonement.

All My Sons relies on coincidence and contrivance. The play works in production, when an audience is more likely to excuse heavy-handedness and yield to the drama's emotional power. But as text, it cannot cover its seams, and a reader may well be disturbed by Kate's casual remark that her husband hasn't been sick in fifteen years—which leads to the discovery of his lie; by Annie's long-concealed letter from Larry, which clears up the doubt concerning his disappearance; and by Keller's sudden remorse and suicide.

Despite these remnants of nineteenth-century conventions, however, and their seeming incompatibility with the twentieth-century realistic play, Miller crafts his drama deftly, drawing for its structure on the retrospective technique that has come to be identified as "Ibsenesque." In such a structure, the past continually intrudes upon the present, and the exposition often sustains itself through the final act, when the critical piece of information necessary for the play's dramatic ending is revealed. Miller found such a structure particularly hospitable for this story, which insists on the consequences of past action. As Miller notes in the introduction to *Collected Plays*, the question was not whether Keller or Chris could ameliorate the consequences of the crime: "The stakes remaining are purely the conscience of Joe Keller and its awakening to the evil he has done, and the conscience of his son in the face of what he has discovered about his father. . . . the structure of the play is designed to bring a man into the direct path of the consequences he has wrought."[2]

Throughout *All My Sons*, Miller works gradually at bringing the audience's level of awareness to that of those in the drama: Keller knows he is responsible for the pilots' deaths; he knows why his wife must continue to believe her son is alive; and he knows that his neighbors know of his guilt. Similarly, Keller's wife, Kate, shares this knowledge. On the other hand, Chris, whose level of awareness coincides with that of the audience, has believed in his father's innocence and tries in earnest to persuade his mother to accept Larry's death. Annie, who returns to the Keller household after several years' absence, has adjusted to the death of her sweetheart, Larry, and is now ready to turn her affections to Chris. She, it turns out, possesses the critical piece of information about Larry's death, which places her above all the other characters in one respect, but, until the play is well under way and her brother George appears, she does not know that her father is serving the prison sentence that is rightfully Keller's. As the play proceeds, providing information to Annie and Chris and, with respect to Larry's death, to Joe and Kate, the audience adjusts its perspectives to accommodate the new evidence, becoming increasingly suspicious of Keller's integrity. With Chris and Annie, it discovers Keller's guilt, and, with Joe and Kate, it learns that Keller's action was responsible for the death of his own son as well.

All My Sons takes place in late August, three and one-half years after the loss of the twenty-one pilots and the report that Larry was missing in action. Within twenty-four hours of play time, the Kellers' lives move from tranquillity to calamity, from ignorance or denial of the truth to discovery or admission. The action takes place in the Kellers' backyard, a typically American setting with trees and lawn and a sheltered cove in which Keller relaxes with the Sunday paper. Neighbors on both sides — Jim and Sue Bayliss and Frank and Lydia Lubey — feel free to stop by to share the paper or to chat, lending assurance of the perfectly normal routine of this family's comfortable life.

But act 1 gradually prepares its characters for the catastrophe that will follow, teasing its audience with sour notes that intrude upon this atmosphere of normality. When Frank stops by, he notices what an audience would also have noticed immediately: the slender apple tree downstage left lies toppled, a casualty of the previous night's storm. Keller and son worry about how Kate will respond to the destruction of the tree the family planted in tribute to Larry. As it turns out, Kate already knows about the tree, having witnessed its fate at four A.M., when a vision of Larry flying high above the house in his plane urged her outside. Kate becomes an important figure in the opening act, creating interest through her stolid refusal to accept Larry's death and her repeated insistence that he may yet return. At her request, Frank has been working on Larry's horoscope, which, if it shows that the fatal day in November was a "favorable" day for Larry, will reinforce her hope. Kate's obsession only deepens when Larry's old girlfriend, Annie, returns for a visit at Chris's invitation; she strenuously opposes an alliance between her second son and the woman she still perceives as "Larry's girl."

The effect of such early interest in Kate and in the developing conflict between her and her son Chris over Annie is to delay the interest the play will gradually but forcefully develop in Keller, who will prove to be the central character—one of the first in a line of strong-willed, self-deluded men who typify Miller's vision of the American family. Such a masculine figurehead is both its backbone and its bane.[3] But there are hints in act 1 that Joe will be at the center of the drama. Bert, one of the neighborhood boys, rushes into the Keller yard speaking of law breakers and law enforcers and begging to see the prison in the Keller basement. Keller knows the terms of the game he has encouraged in the neighborhood, but he laughingly sends the boy off without showing him the jail. Speaking delightedly about this game to his wife, Keller explains that the kids took an interest in him when he returned from the penitentiary, but then they began confusing the former inmate with the detective. Kate is quick to correct Keller, suggesting it was not *they* who got confused. The game her husband plays has much to do with his own history, which naturally becomes part of the discussion with the long-absent Annie. Deever, whom Annie and her brother have disowned and whom Keller calls a "little man," is in jail, the consequence of Keller's deliberate confusion of the facts. The criminal became the law enforcer, misrepresented the facts, and assumed the role of the innocent. Upon his return from jail following his exoneration, Keller got out of his car at the corner so he could walk the distance of the block, his head held defiantly high against the neighbors' scorn. But since then, poker games and neighborly rapport have been restored, and the criminal has become the pillar of society.

Similarly, Chris speaks of his days in the army, where he led a corps of men who displayed uncommon friendship and loyalty, defending their colleagues even at the expense of their own lives. Because he escaped the fate of so many of them, Chris feels a vague sense of guilt over his own survival. Though too early in the play to make the connection explicitly, this introspective moment offers a contrast to the guilt-free Keller, who has unconscionably let Deever take the blame. And then Kate responds twice with a disturbing anger, an insistence so impassioned as to be suspicious. She reprimands the child for believing there is a basement jail, then returns to Keller's curious question, the central question of the play, "What have I got to hide?" And when Kate defends her belief in Larry's survival, she reminds her husband, with uncommon intensity, that he above all has got to believe.

By the end of act 1, the audience is sure the play will be Keller's and is anxious about the turn of events. Annie's brother, George, having traveled seven hundred miles from New York to Columbus to tell his father of Annie's impending marriage, telephones. He is coming to the Kellers' home, apparently with some new and disturbing knowledge. Alone on stage, Kate and Keller react. Kate fears George's arrival and cautions her husband to be smart. Keller is angry, arrogant, and self-assured. The call redirects attention to the case of the cracked cylinders and to the question of what Keller has to hide.

Miller's second act offers an effective balance of bitterness and sweetness, of anxiety and relief, prolonging its two dramatic questions: How will Annie react to George's belief in his father's innocence—will she still marry into the family that is "covered with blood"—and how will Keller react—will he admit he framed his partner? Was he, in fact, responsible for the shipment of the cylinders? The act takes place later that day, at twilight. Chris is sawing off the broken apple tree and suggesting to his mother that without it there is more light. The atmosphere is one of anticipation: they are waiting for the arrival of George, whom Jim has gone to fetch at the station. Chris, assured in his belief that the family has nothing to hide, seems unconcerned, but Kate is overreacting, pleading with Chris to protect them. She fears the case will be reopened and that Deever's story—that Keller made him do it—will prevail. Near hysteria, she begs Chris to help them—and to send Annie home, for she is of the Deever clan, which hates them. Keller, by contrast, is not worrying, or at least he is expressing his concern more passively— through sleeping.

In the moments before George's arrival, though, even as Keller sleeps, the father-son conflict so familiar to readers of Miller begins to take form. Annie has a chance conversation with neighbor Sue about Chris, which is especially revealing. She dislikes Chris for his idealism and proceeds to impute a fundamental dishonesty to him since he, despite his "holiness," still works in his father's business. Clearly, the neighbors have never believed in Keller's innocence and now resent not only his freedom at the expense of Deever but Chris's acceptance of the tainted firm as the source of his livelihood, even as he silently preaches perfection.

Annie, upset, immediately confronts Chris with Sue's opinions, which Chris dismisses as just that. Chris, after all, is attached to his parents, and his love for his father is particularly—and reciprocally—intense. Keller, in fact, has worked all his life for his sons, and, with Larry gone, his hopes rest completely in Chris. Earlier in the play, when Chris appealed to Keller to side with him in his desire to marry Annie, he threatened to leave the business if Keller did not support his cause, and the astonished father capitulated. Keller's need to leave his life's effort as a legacy to his son anticipates a similarly intense—and misdirected—desire in Miller's later central character, Willy Loman. As with the deluded salesman, Keller must have his son be heir or see the commitment of his life invalidated. With Willy, a dream is at stake, but with Keller, Chris's participation in the family business is all that keeps the older man from being a murderer. When, later in the play, Keller confesses his treachery, he justifies it in terms of the prospect of losing his life's work, of robbing himself of the legacy he has promised his sons. He shipped out the risky cylinder heads so he could buy time to prove his business viable and to preserve the business for Chris. Yet Keller still calls the firm J. O. Keller, not J. O. Keller & Son; despite Chris's commitment to the firm, his name has not yet been attached to it. George makes a point of this a bit later, understanding that, though Chris may defend his father as head of the "Holy Family," what is at least an unconscious doubt has prevented him from becoming a partner. Chris can barely assimilate his father's later plea: "I did it for you."

Just before George's arrival, then, a gossipy neighbor has set up the father-son relationship that is central to a play that is, finally, a story of fidelity and belief. Bert believes there is a prison under the Keller house, despite Kate's testimony to the contrary. Yet Kate holds a more dangerous, adult delusion: that her husband is innocent, her son Larry alive. In the first instance, she knows that belief in Keller's innocence necessitates a lie, and she has, for over three years, pretended to others what she has never been able to pretend to herself. But believing in Larry's survival is a bit more manageable, for she has no proof to the contrary. Over the years, though, Kate has connected the events so inextricably that her profession of faith in Larry has become a surrogate expression of faith in her husband. Like Keller, she serves the image of the American family as sacrosanct; neither is willing to admit that their Holy Family is headed by a moral weakling, a man whose culpability is compounded by his refusal to admit his wrong. Neither Keller nor Kate is so self-deluded as to believe their own protestations of innocence, but their belief in the sanctity of the Keller family motivates their perpetuation of the lie. Chris is heir to his parents' principles and morality, yet, being an honest man and an idealist, he can believe only in the purity of his father's behavior. His is the more treacherous kind of self-delusion, for Chris believes religiously in the lie. He never suspected his father's guilt because he could not accommodate that guilt with his vision of self or of family. With his parents, he has joined in the lie—though clearly without any awareness that he is doing so. The neighbors, by contrast, are aware of Keller's guilt, of Kate's cover-up, and of Chris's ignorance by design; they admire Keller's cunning but detest his morality. Yet still, in deference to some abstract concept of neighborliness, they chat with the Kellers and even pretend to trust Joe at cards. Only Annie and George seem to accept the loss of faith attendant upon their father's conviction. They assume the law is right and disown their father as a moral weakling who has committed an unconscionable crime.

The play is a web, then, of homespun fidelities, of faith placed and misplaced, a network of belief that, like the apple tree, snaps under pressure. And the arrival of George begins the weakening of

several of the strands, for it prompts Sue to speak contemptuously
to Annie of Chris's "phoney idealism," and it reveals the restoration
of George's belief in his father.

Deever, of course, has been the victim of the Keller family's
deception, and now George has just returned from telling his father
that Annie is about to marry into that family. George is himself a
lawyer, a man who should see clearly the difference between right
and wrong but who has himself been duped for years, too ready to
accept Joe's story over his father's. Tellingly, he enters the Keller
household wearing his father's hat—and he has come to take Annie
home. This time, George believes his father's story. After three and
a half years, he now sees his father as Keller's victim and refuses to
allow the moral taint of the Keller family to claim his sister. But,
even here, Miller does things gradually: though vehement and bitter
when he enters, George falls prey to nostalgia, to Kate's charm, and
to the weaknesses he knows his father possesses. Joe's tactic is to
welcome George with warmth, arranging a meeting with Lydia, his
former girlfriend; to discredit Deever by cataloging other moments
of his weakness; and to extend himself generously, offering Deever a
position with the firm when in a year or two he gets out of jail. Kate
works at George's sense of nostalgia; the two were always friends,
and she has remembered to provide him with his favorite grape
juice.

The seduction is too much for George, and the bitter reunion
turns into a sweet one, with talk of childhood experiences and
preparations for the evening meal. Relaxed and appeased, George
confesses he never felt at home anywhere but there. He compliments
Kate on her youthful appearance and tells Joe he is "amazingly the
same." Keller responds by saying he has no time to get sick, and then
Kate, endorsing her husband's pride in his good health, speaks the
fatal line: "He hasn't been laid up in fifteen years," breaking the
spell. Despite Joe's immediate qualification—"Except my flu during
the war"—George is alert and challenging, for it was Keller's alleged
illness that kept him from the plant on the day the cracked cylinder
heads came off the line. Ironically, at the moment when the Kellers
are threatened so darkly and so inescapably, at the moment when
Kate's worst fears are about to be realized, Miller brings Frank

onstage with the announcement that he has completed Larry's horoscope: November 25 was a "favorable" day; Larry must be alive.

But Larry is about to die, for Kate's belief in him need not be
sustained beyond the revelation of her husband's guilt, which
George's anger now presages. Kate and George both want Annie to
leave, but Chris reacts with passion, prohibiting further mention of
Larry and directing George to leave. Annie joins Chris in telling her
brother to go.

In the quarrel between Kate and Chris that ensues, Kate finally
reveals the truth:

MOTHER: Your brother's alive, darling, because if he's dead, your father
killed him. Do you understand me now? As long as you live, that boy is
alive. God does not let a son be killed by his father. Now you see, don't
you? Now you see. (*CP*, p. 114)

Defeated, Keller pleads that his son never flew a P-40, then
justifies his decision: forty years of his life were at risk the day he
ordered the cylinders shipped; he took the chance for Chris's sake.
But Chris's sense of moral responsibility, unlike his father's, extends
beyond the personal, beyond the family to the larger family of
which he felt a part during the war.

Father and son collide over an issue that will resonate through
Miller's plays: the conflict between the social and the personal. In
this play, as in others that Miller will later write, a man's personal
integrity, even his survival, depends on his denial of his social responsibility. Had Keller not wanted so desperately to pass on the
family business to his son, he might not have been so profit-oriented
as a businessman. He might have halted production of the cylinders
and not met the government contract, despite the financial consequence. But, yielding to individual and family pride, he risked pro-
cessing the faulty parts and lost the bet. Then, faced again with a
moral crisis—whether to confess his complicity or look to Deever as
a scapegoat—he chose the latter, necessitating a life of deception
afterwards. Once Chris understands what his father has done, once
he has identified the heinous consequences of Keller's having placed
the personal above the social, the final act moves inexorably toward
restitution of the social order through the offender's death. Keller

leaves in his wake the broken relationship between Annie and Chris,
a dead son, and a family fallen like the apple tree; the sense of a
moral and social order prevails.

Keller's guilt established, the dramatic question shifts from
"What does Joe Keller have to hide?" to "What will happen now
that everyone knows?" Act 2, like act 1, ends with a heavy curtain,
Chris pounding his fist on his father's shoulder and weeping, not
knowing what to do.

Several hours pass during the interlude between acts, bringing
the play's action to two A.M. the following day. Act 3 opens with the
contemplative Kate rocking on the porch chair, in moonlight. She is
waiting for Chris to return. Jim talks with her as she rocks, revealing that the neighbors always knew, and assuring her that Chris will
come back. While they wait, the elder Kellers try to salvage what is
left of their lives, Joe turning meekly to Kate for guidance and she
counseling yet another lie: if he told Chris he was willing to go to
prison, Chris surely would not ask him to go, but perhaps he would
forgive him. Even now, Keller cannot accept responsibility, self-
righteously asking what there was that Chris needed to forgive.
Acknowledging Kate as the accomplice that she undoubtedly has
been, he characteristically shifts the blame once again, faulting her
for wanting money. Kate sees that her husband is trying to exoner-
ate himself on familial grounds: "Joe, Joe . . . it don't excuse it that
you did it for the family," but Keller insists, "It's got to excuse it!"

The moment is more critical for Keller than the revelation of
his guilt in the earlier act. As Miller notes in the introduction to
Collected Plays,

Joe Keller's trouble, in a word, is not that he cannot tell right from wrong
but that his cast of mind cannot admit that he, personally, has any viable
connection with his world, his universe, or his society. He is not a partner
in society, but an incorporated member, so to speak, and you cannot sue
personally the officers of a corporation. (*CP*, p. 19)

Keller has always believed in the family as an autonomous entity
and the highest principle:

Nothin's bigger than that. . . . I'm his father and he's my son, and if there's
something bigger than that I'll put a bullet in my head! (*CP*, p. 120).

Within the hour, Keller does put a bullet in his head, in a gesture that both insists on his own belief in family and tentatively acknowledges that his sons, Chris and Larry, may be right in seeing something bigger. Unwilling to relinquish his belief, Keller argues with Chris when he returns, defending himself as a man no worse than others. Ironically, Chris never measured him against other men, never even saw him as a man but only as his father, and until the revelation of act 2, Chris's vision of Keller coincided with his abstract ideal. His philosophy of family affirmed his father's, but now Chris understands what he had known in his army days and had ignored—intentionally or unintentionally—since the court case: that there is something bigger than the family. It is a belief endorsed by brother Larry, through the letter he wrote to Annie on the day of his suicide, which Chris now reads aloud. Larry could not live with the shame of his father's involvement in the deaths of his fellow men. Keller understands that to Larry, "they were all my sons. And I guess they were, I guess they were."

In "The Family in Modern Drama," Miller avers that all great plays deal with a single problem:

How may a man make of the outside world a home? How and in what ways must he struggle, what must he strive to change and overcome within himself and outside himself if he is to find the safety, the surroundings of love, the ease of soul, the sense of identity and honor which, evidently, all men have connected in their memories with the idea of family?[4]

By the time Keller has the capacity to acknowledge his membership in a larger, social family, whose principles, when in conflict with those of the private family, must prevail, he has already so violated its moral assumptions that even a prison sentence will not absolve him. To Miller, Keller threatens society not because he has sold faulty parts to the military but because that crime has "roots in a certain relationship of the individual to society, and to a certain indoctrination he embodies, which, if dominant, can mean a jungle existence for all of us no matter how high our buildings soar" (*CP*, p. 19).

If there is hope for redemption among the remaining Kellers at play's end, that hope rests in Chris, who ends the act sobbing at

Kate's feet as she frees him to live. Chris will leave the Keller household, he will not marry Annie, and he will renew the lesson of his
army days that his father—and Willy Loman after him—had such a
difficult time learning. For Miller, the struggle between father and
son "for recognition and forgiveness," in both *All My Sons* and
Death of a Salesman, is insufficient: "But when it extends itself out
of the family circle and into society, it broaches those questions of
social status, social honor and recognition, which expand its vision
and lift it out of the merely particular toward the fate of the general-
ity of men."[5]

3

◆◆◆

Death of a Salesman

When Walter Goodman reviewed the 1975 revival of *Death of a Salesman*, in which George C. Scott replaced Lee J. Cobb as the self-deluded drummer, he claimed that the play, though applauded in 1949 as the great American tragedy, might well mean more in 1975. Goodman argues that the sympathetic reception of so unmitigated a failure as Willy Loman could be expected from a people who had lived through the Great Depression and World War II, but identification with this loser of a salesman could not have lasted beyond the two-hour life of the play. For this audience was on its way to becoming the Affluent Society; in 1949, Willy Loman was "an anachronism, a relic of a Depression mentality." By 1975, however, America had again become a society ready to acknowledge that "attention must be paid," even to this unlikable, inept failure, whose condition rather than personality was moving. For the 1975 audience had lived through an unpopular, unnecessary war, which brought none of the enthusiasm or the nationalism of World War II; and it was disillusioned with two decades of an energetic prosperity that could not pause for failures nor accommodate a man who yearned to plant seeds or look at the moon.[1]

In 1984, Willy Loman appeared once again on the Broadway stage, this time a bit thinner and a bit smaller—more like the original "shrimp" Miller had created than the "walrus" into which Willy was metamorphosed when Lee J. Cobb was cast. Dustin Hoffman's portrayal of Willy was powerful and convincing, suggesting that the method actor had clearly found some coincidence between himself and the character that enabled him to create the role. But where America was in the mid-1980s did not seem to concern the critics. *Death of a Salesman* was no longer being viewed as time-bound

commentary on capitalism and its victims, and audience response
was not being judged in terms of economic or social circumstance.
Miller's play had clearly earned its author's description of it as a
play that raises "questions . . . whose answers define humanity,"[2] a
description dramatically endorsed in 1983 when the play opened at
the Beijing People's Art Theater in China.

That production, the first in China of an American play directed by an American, challenged the assumption that *Salesman* was
culture-bound, meeting with enthusiastic responses in a country
where peasants constitute 90 percent of the population and where
there are no salesmen. Speaking of the opening in *"Salesman" in
Beijing*, Miller noticed the odd laughs, the cruel laughs, beneath
which he sensed "a comprehension of Willy's character, a recognition. Which I suppose means they share these embarrassing
weaknesses?"[3] Harry Moses, producer of the Bill Moyers show on
PBS, which ran a special program on the production of *Death of a
Salesman* in Beijing, told Miller the day after opening night that the
last shot on the program would be of a young Chinese who spoke
English, saying that "China was full of Willys, dreamers of the
dream."[4]

But the problem with Willy—aside from his self-delusion, his
ineptness, his self-pity, his misplaced pride, and his fraudulent morality—is that he has dreamed the wrong dream. About to be fired
from his job, Willy cries out to the young upstart Howard, "You
can't eat the orange and throw the peel away—a man is not a piece
of fruit!" Though only the peel of Willy's dream remains, he refuses
to discard it, deluding himself into believing that the dream of being
a salesman with green velvet slippers, who was not only liked but
well liked by the hundreds who mourned his death, was right for
him.

There may well be no character in modern drama more memo-
rable than Willy Loman. The image of the tired salesman, valise in
hand, shoulders sloping, suit jacket hanging loosely about his weary frame, which appeared on the jacket of the Viking edition of the
play for years, has sustained its power in the imagination of the
theatergoing public. It has become a symbol of the pursuer of the
American—and the universal—dream who met with the harsh consequences of not being able to keep up. Willy Loman is indeed a low

man; no tragic hero of high degree, he is circumstantially and psychologically down. Surrounded by high-rise apartment buildings that deflect the sun from the backyard, Willy's little house in Brooklyn stands as a symbol of time past, when the world still had room for vegetable gardens and for salesmen who carried on their trade on the strength of a smile. There is a collective guilt in Willy's failure in which every theatergoer participates; it is a guilt occasioned by the knowledge that society cannot accommodate its failures in a system that relentlessly demands success.

Willy is hardly unique in Miller's early Broadway plays. He is of a breed with his predecessor, Joe Keller, who would not stop production of the faulty cylinder heads because it would put him out of business and cancel out his dream. Both fathers of two sons, Willy and Joe want to succeed for their sons' sake, want to pass on the tokens of success to their heirs. Neither can entertain the possibility of his sons' refusing the legacy, and each has justified his life's labor, with its attendant misjudgments, in family terms. Like Joe, Willy has a supportive wife who makes her husband's self-delusion possible. She is a woman who loves her husband and commits herself to him even at the expense of her personal integrity, the nourishing mother-wife without whom neither head of the household could survive.

In the introduction to *Collected Plays*, Miller describes the genesis of these two immensely successful plays as taking place in the many months of thinking about his first professionally produced drama, *The Man Who Had All the Luck*. While he was lying on the beach, "a simple shift of relationships came to mind": "What I saw . . . was that two of the characters, who had been friends in the previous drafts, were logically brothers and had the same father." The playwright enjoyed a "fullness of feeling" when he began writing of the father-son relationship: "The crux of *All My Sons*, which would not be written until nearly three years later, was formed; and the roots of *Death of a Salesman* were sprouted" (*CP*, pp. 14–15).

When *All My Sons* took shape, it followed the construction principles of Ibsenesque realism, progressing in a tightly controlled chronology with one scene leading causally to the next and transitional moments bridging scenes; as Miller describes it, the play

proceeds "a stitch at a time . . . in order to weave a tapestry." But
when the playwright conceived *Salesman*, he wanted a form with "a
kind of moment-to-moment wildness" that *All My Sons* did not
have:

> The first image that occurred to me which was to result in *Death of a
> Salesman* was of an enormous face the height of the proscenium arch which
> would appear and then open up, and we would see the inside of a man's
> head. In fact, *The Inside of His Head* was the first title. . . . The image was
> in direct opposition to the method of *All My Sons*—a method one might
> call linear or eventual in that one fact or incident creates the necessity for
> the next. The *Salesman* image was from the beginning absorbed with the
> concept that nothing in life comes "next" but that everything exists together
> and at the same time within us; that there is no past to be "brought for-
> ward" in a human being, but that he is his past at every moment. . . .
> I wished to create a form which, in itself as a form, would literally be
> the process of Willy Loman's way of mind. (*CP*, pp. 23–24)

Miller discarded the idea of a colossal head that would open up
to reveal its possessor's thoughts, but he achieved psychological
intimacy through a series of reveries that slipped in and out of the
present action, suggesting that, for Willy, the past and the present
were one. While the set is stylized rather than realistic, the present
action of the play takes place within defined boundaries, indicated
throughout by the Loman home and, for the "city scenes" in act 2,
by properties evoking the offices of Wagner and Company, Willy's
employer; the offices of Charley, his neighbor; and a restaurant
where Willy meets his sons.

The play begins with Willy returning from an aborted sales trip
to New England, mystified by his inability to keep the car from
driving off the road. Apparently, Willy has been in such a circumstance before, causing his devoted wife considerable concern, and
now the two decide that in the morning Willy will ask Howard
Wagner for a transfer to New York. Since Willy knew the elder
Wagner well, he is confident that the son, acknowledging his father's friendship with Willy, will honor his request. His needs, after
all, are modest, and he has a debt to claim for years ago opening up
the New England territory to the firm.

Willy's son, Biff, is making one of his occasional visits, having returned from the ranch in Texas where he worked. His brother, Happy, holds a low-level position as a junior assistant manager in New York and spends most of his money womanizing. Neither of the sons understands the crisis his aging father is going through; only Linda knows how dangerously close to suicide Willy is. Supporting, flattering, patronizing her husband, she fiercely asserts his worth, providing the spiritual glue that holds together the rickety frame.

During the course of the play, Willy gets himself fired, even as his son, Biff, fails to consummate a business deal that had no possibility of materializing in the first place. The salesman winds up killing himself, not in defeat but in the euphoric hope of furthering his dream through his sons, who will collect twenty-thousand dollars in insurance money. Willy dies endorsing the lie that has sustained his life.

The real action of the play, though, is internal, taking place in the several reveries that consume Willy at critical moments. In Willy's reveries, which are dramatized on the apron of the stage, the set becomes imaginary, with Willy recreating moments that took place in the Loman home and backyard and in a hotel room in Boston, involving not only characters from the present action but brother Ben and the woman with whom Willy had an affair. Willy slips into the past whenever he is confronted with a crisis too difficult for him to accommodate and, finally, when he needs to make a decision about suicide.

Whenever Biff comes to visit, Willy is particularly vulnerable. As Linda explains, he is pleased at first to hear that his son is coming, but when he sees Biff he cannot remain in conversation with him for a moment without a quarrel. Upset that at age thirty-four Biff has still not found a profession but keeps moving from one odd ranch or farm job to another, Willy keeps expressing his need to have his son be successful. Willy's first reverie is occasioned both by Biff's visit and by his own failure to make it to New England. It is an ideal vision of how things were when the boys were in high school, when they idolized their father and when Biff was a football star. But Biff's life ended the day of the championship game at Ebbets Field—and Willy claims not to understand why. In fact, as his later conversation with Bernard reveals, Biff did nothing of worth after that moment of triumph and burned his University of Virginia sneakers after a visit to Boston to ask his father to plead with a math teacher to give him a passing grade.

A later reverie in act 2, initiated by Happy and Biff's teaming up with two women in a restaurant when they were supposed to have dinner with their father, reveals that, when Biff arrived in Boston unannounced, he discovered a woman in Willy's hotel room. Though Willy has never consciously admitted the effect of the encounter on his son, the insistence of the event as memory suggests that, were Willy honest with himself, he would understand how damaged Biff was by his discovery that the father he admired was an ordinary, fallible man.

Biff's friend Bernard, whom Willy sees going off to Washington, DC to argue a case before the Supreme Court, has a special place in Willy's memory, as the boy who applied himself in school and got good grades, who couldn't give Biff the answers on the Regents math exam, and who, though not "well-liked," has become a family man and a success. But Willy's sons, who had bodies like Adonises, who, when they stole lumber or a football, received their father's commendation for initiative, and who invested their energy in sports and in being well-liked—all with the endorsement and encouragement of their father—remain unmarried and unsuccessful. But in this respect, Willy's memories only confirm what his present actions reveal: he has lived by a morality that is less than worthy of respect and that nurtured dishonesty in his boys.

At sixty, Willy may be entitled to some self-delusion, but, even when the boys were in high school, Willy was pretending to Linda that he earned more money than he did, giving a woman in Boston new silk stockings while Linda sat mending hers, packaging dishonesty as wisdom in a life plan for his sons. Willy's reveries contribute poignantly to the characterization of a man unable to admit failure but passionately defensive of every mistake and misdeed he has committed.

So also do they raise a major question of credibility, filtered as they are through the mind of a man on the edge of a breakdown, prepared at any moment to end a life that, by both society's standards and Willy's, has amounted to little. When Willy supervised the simonizing of the Chevy, did his sons appreciate his advice?

When he announced that those boys idolized him, was he engaging in wishful thinking? Did Biff ever tell his father he would break out for a touchdown at Ebbets Field just for him? Indeed, did Biff ever think enough of his father to respond so dramatically to the Boston affair? He himself seems to join brother Happy in the indiscriminate pursuit of women, with no moral reservations; Willy may be haunted by an image that, ironically, he need never have had to deny. His reveries, in short, may well be more—or less—than recall; they may be Willy's way of restructuring history and self.

The possibility becomes especially pronounced in Willy's visions of Ben, who clearly appears as Willy's imaginative version of his brother. Willy, after all, has not seen his brother since Ben invited him to Alaska a quarter of a century earlier; yet Ben appears in Willy's reveries as a sixty-year-old man. As Sister M. Bettina suggests in a provocative piece on Willy's brother, Ben "takes shape less as person external to Willy than as a projection of his personality."[5] In the present scenes, only Linda mentions him, and then in response to Willy; he may, in fact, be Willy's invention, the fictional model he has created in order to assure himself that dreams are worth dreaming and that, in becoming a salesman, he chose to follow the right dream. Years earlier, Willy might have gone to Alaska with Ben, but he chose instead to conquer the New England territory. He has wondered since about the road not taken and looked to Ben for assurance that he has not made a mistake. At his first appearance, Willy defends his life in Brooklyn to brother Ben and boasts of his sons' physical prowess, shamelessly seeking Ben's endorsement, which he receives: "William, you're being first-rate with your boys. Outstanding, manly chaps!" Ben's parting comment of how he got rich quick through rugged individualism leaves Willy enthusiastic: "That's just the spirit I want to imbue them with! To walk into a jungle! I was right! I was right! I was right!" Willy comes to his own judgment but rejoices in Ben's approval.

Ben returns to Willy's mind when the salesman is fired, when Willy recreates the moment of his refusal: he did not go to Alaska because he was "building something with this firm." This time, Ben offers the contrary reaction: "There's a new continent at your doorstep, William. You could walk out rich. Rich!" Willy shouts after

him, "We'll do it here, Ben! You hear me? We're gonna do it here!"
even as he sits in Howard's office, without a job.

Whether real or imagined, Ben is a projection of Willy's own
psyche, a device Willy has found necessary in order to test his
yearnings and, in effect, argue with himself. It is particularly telling
that Willy's final psychic departure from the present takes him not
into the past, as all his other reveries do, but into a fictional present
in which he can discuss the future — more specifically, suicide — with
Ben.

Part of Willy, of course, does not want to go through with the
act, and that part speaks first through Ben, appealing to his pride
and telling him to make sure the sacrifice is not offered in vain. But
the part of Willy that wants to drive his car off the road and wants
to leave Biff the insurance money, speaks finally with certainty
through Ben: "And twenty thousand — that *is* something one can feel
with the hand, it is there." His plan endorsed by Ben, Willy finally
follows his brother's path into the jungle: "Oh, Ben, that's the
whole beauty of it! I see it like a diamond, shining in the dark, hard
and rough, that I can pick up and touch in my hand." His sons will
have the insurance money; Willy's dream has paid off. The dead
Willy joins his brother Ben, who perhaps died several weeks earlier,
as Willy tells Charley, or who perhaps died just now, with Willy.

Over the years, much of the criticism surrounding *Death of a
Salesman* has measured Willy in terms of Miller's essay on "Tragedy
and the Common Man."[6] In that now-famous statement on the
possibilities for tragedy in the modern world, Miller offers necessary revisions to Aristotle's observations on Greek tragedy and defends the legitimacy of the common man as hero. Acknowledging
that the modern world may have fewer heroes than earlier ages and
fewer possibilities for heroic action, Miller speaks of the modern
tragic hero as one who is willing to lay down his life if need be in
order to preserve his dignity. The playwright speaks almost exclu-
sively in terms of commitment, curiously removing the tragic hero
from any relationship to a commonly agreed-upon moral structure
that dictates the principles to which commitments are made and by
which their admirability and rightness might be assessed. He mentions nothing of the tragic hero's self-awareness, nothing of the
recognition — always too late — that precedes disaster.

As so monumental a figure, Willy Loman deserves scrutiny in terms of both Miller's concept of tragedy and Aristotle's, but only if Miller's prevails can he qualify as a tragic hero. And then the description must be so radically altered that Aristotle's assessment of the effect of the hero's death on the audience must be ignored. For our reaction to Willy, as George Jean Nathan points out, is "like the experience we suffer in contemplating on the highways a run-over and killed dog":[7] there is pathos, perhaps, but no elevation of spirit; there is no expansive sense of the possibilities of humankind, only an acute perception of its limitations. Had Willy, like Oedipus, come to understand his errors, to see through his delusion to a clear vision of self, an audience might have been left with the full sense of tragic irony that comes when a tragic hero acquires self-knowledge only at a point when he cannot stop the consequences of his earlier ignorance. It might have been left with the feeling that there was yet potential in Willy, who might finally have abandoned his futile dream and pursued a life of gardening or carpentry. But Willy dies in service of the dream he has worshipped all his life, the dream that has nurtured a vision of self that bears little resemblance to reality, and he leaves that dream as legacy to his sons, who have no more chance at success than Willy has had. Willy's weary form casts an immense shadow over all of modern drama, but because he goes to his death without the wisdom of self-discovery, he remains a pathetic "low man."

Yet Willy's failure to evoke the conventional tragic response should in no way diminish his power as a dramatic character. Willy's mistake, Miller says—in a statement somewhat inconsistent with his identification of personal commitment as the measure of the modern tragic hero—is that he violated a law of society, which says that society's failures have no right to live. Finding himself up against a modern world of high-rise apartment buildings and tape recorders that give permanence to voices with nothing to say, Willy can only remember Dave Singleman, who did business from a telephone in a hotel room and was honored with ceremony and respect when, at eighty-four, he died. For Willy, there is an unbridgeable chasm between Dave Singleman's world, which was the world in which Willy operated when he was younger, and a world that can no longer accommodate his outmoded approach to business and to life. Sales have little to do with friendship or personal style, and Willy does not know how to function in an aggressively success-oriented world: "In those days there was personality in it, Howard. There was respect, and comradeship, and gratitude in it. Today, it's all cut and dried." Things in Willy's world are breaking down—the refrigerator, the car, the plumbing, the leaky roof—and Willy is too. Boxed in by high-rise apartment buildings, by "bricks and windows, windows and bricks," Willy complains that "[you] gotta break your neck to see a star in this yard." And so little sun reaches Willy's lot that nothing will grow. In his more honest moments, Willy generates a vision of life quite apart from the twentieth-century technology that has pervaded and invaded his life. Longing for grass and sunshine, a pastoral ideal, he tells Linda that one day they will have a place in the country, where he can raise vegetables and chickens.

Significantly, Willy's last action before his suicide is a pathetic attempt to plant seeds in his darkened garden where nothing can grow. This is the legacy he would like to leave his sons, but he settles for the twenty-thousand dollars insurance money, which only misdirects him once again and seals the dream he should never have had. But just as significantly, Biff, who has lived on a horse ranch in Texas and himself loves the outdoors, comes to understand the toxicity of Willy's dream, both for his father and for himself. Having returned to Bill Oliver, a former employer, to ask for a loan so the two brothers can set up a sporting goods store—a loan he has no chance of securing—Biff, in frustration, steals Oliver's pen. But as he is running down the stairs, he has the recognition that his father should have had:

I ran down eleven flights with a pen in my hand today. And suddenly I stopped, you hear me? And in the middle of that office building, do you hear this? I stopped in the middle of that building and I saw—the sky. I saw the things that I love in this world. The work and the food and time to sit and smoke. And I looked at the pen and said to myself, what the hell am I grabbing this for? Why am I trying to become what I don't want to be? What am I doing in an office, making a contemptuous, begging fool of myself, when all I want is out there, waiting for me the minute I say I know who I am! (*CP*, p. 217)

Unlike Willy, Biff still has the possibility for epiphany and the capacity for change.

Willy's epiphany, if it may be called that, is pitiful by comparison. Seeing his son in tears, Willy is astonished and concludes, in elation, that Biff likes him. Linda quickly embellishes the judgment: "He loves you, Willy!", and Happy endorses it: "Always did, Pop." But Willy has heard only Biff's sobs; he ignores his son's plea for him to "take that phony dream and burn it before something happens"; within moments, he is talking with brother Ben about suicide. Ironically, this moment of greatest promise for the relationship between father and son and for Willy's own self-knowledge finds expression in Willy's decision to drive his car off the road. As Miller puts it, he is ready to bestow "'power' on his posterity," to sell "his last asset, himself, for the price of his insurance policy" (*CP*, p. 34). Biff's show of insight only further distorts Willy's vision: if Biff loves him, Biff has forgiven him for the Boston affair, and his fatherhood is restored; if Biff loves him, Biff wants to be what Willy wants him to be—he too worships the dream. Willy's interpretation of Biff's breakdown seduces him into a deluded death gesture that only compounds the waste of his life.

Willy's readiness to die for the sake of his dream affirms the personality of a man who has always seen himself as invulnerable, in large part because his wife, Linda, convinced him he was so. A forgiving and devoted woman, who acknowledges to her sons that her husband is not the greatest man who ever lived but who loves him dearly and insists he commands respect—or at least attention— Linda fortifies Willy with encouraging words and praise, reviving his spirits whenever they sag. When Willy's commissions are not so substantial as they might have been, even in earlier years, Linda allows him to pretend he made more than he did and praises him for his achievement. When Willy tells her of how he lost his temper and hit a salesman in the face when the man called him a walrus, Linda does not reproach him for his behavior but tells him that, to her, he is the handsomest man in the world. When Willy keeps driving the car off the road, though she knows of his death wish, she tries to excuse the action by suggesting he needs an eye examination or a good rest.

Even when Linda discovers the rubber hose in the basement,

hidden behind a pipe for the day that Willy can no longer endure, the faithful wife neither confronts him nor removes the hose, knowing Willy depends on her thinking that his strength cannot falter. Managing the household, Linda has been the practical wife, mending stockings, stretching dollars, and ironically, making the final mortgage payment just when Willy dies. But in managing her husband, she has treated him as her hero, giving him little opportunity to be less.

Willy, finally, is tired. He is tired of traveling to New England to be rejected, tired of borrowing money from Charley to pay his bills, tired of hassling his worthless sons when Biff's friend Bernard is arguing a case before the Supreme Court. Willy is world-weary, knowing, like Macbeth, that the accoutrements of old age—friends, trust, security—are not his. Yet he never understands why.

Ultimately, Willy is victim neither of a society that makes unreasonable demands nor of a wife who encourages illusion; he is victim neither of an insensitive son nor of a worthless one nor of his one friend and financial redeemer, Charley. Ultimately, Willy Loman, like all men, is a free agent, self-centered, self-deluded, self-destructive—but responsible. As he continues relentlessly to insist upon the single truth that has shaped his life and prescribed his death, an audience loses its capacity for admiration and respect, wanting instead to take this insufferable old man by the sagging shoulders and shake some sense into him. But even those audience members who know that Willy deserves what he gets are overwhelmed by pathos as they join the handful of mourners in the requiem, horribly aware of the coincidences between Willy's character and their own. Willy Loman may not have had the capacity or the strength to see himself, but for two generations he has been responsible for our seeing ourselves through him.

4

•••

The Crucible

Though *Death of a Salesman* won Miller a second New York Drama Critics' Circle Award and a first Pulitzer Prize, before turning to his next original dramatic effort, *The Crucible*, Miller adapted Ibsen's 1882 play, *An Enemy of the People*. The drama held several understandable attractions for Miller, whose own work revealed his respect for Ibsen's technique and who, with Ibsen, saw drama as an agent of social change. In the preface to his adaptation, Miller celebrates Ibsen's "insistence, his utter conviction, that he is going to say what he has to say, and that the audience, by God, is going to listen."[1] Miller's characterization of Ibsen not simply as the creator of a drama of ideas but as one unwilling to silence or even moderate those ideas suggests the earlier playwright's kinship with his own characters, those who, despite all odds and despite all urgings, pursue their individual beliefs. The stubbornly insistent Dr. Stockmann, who, with Ibsen, holds on to his megaphone to announce what he believes is right, is recognizable and repeatable in the Ibsen canon and is, for Miller, a prototype.

Yet Miller's insistent heroes remain curiously separate from Ibsen's, who uniformly win an audience's respect. Dr. Stockmann is a character eminently deserving of admiration, a man of strength and a model of one unwilling to compromise the truth. Miller's heroes share their predecessor's personal commitment, but, in the case of both Joe Keller and Willy Loman—and Eddie Carbone as well—the men are personally wrong. An audience sees their actions against a backdrop of a society that will not accommodate a personal morality that differs from its own but sees as well the heroes' egregious faults. Though Miller's heroes and Ibsen's share the same passion in their personal commitments, an audience assessing their moral position in a societal context scorns in Miller what it admires in Ibsen. Dr. Stockmann's life is a sacrifice; Joe's, Willy's, and Eddie's deaths are a waste.

Miller's wish to adapt *An Enemy of the People* may at least be explained in part by his interest in Ibsen's protagonist, who fits the description Robert Brustein offers in *The Theatre of Revolt*: Stockmann is a "fanatical individualist defending the safety of the community," a "defiant aristocrat of the will worrying over the happiness of the average man."[2] Though Ibsen explains this superiority not as an aristocracy of birth or even of the intellect but of character, Miller still excises those lines:

> I have taken as justification for removing those examples which no longer prove the theme—examples I believe Ibsen would have removed were he alive today. . . . In light of genocide, the holocaust that has swept our world on the wings of the black ideology of racism, it is inconceivable that Ibsen would insist today that certain individuals are by breeding, or race, or "innate" qualities superior to others or possessed of the right to dictate to others.[3]

Having deflated Stockmann's propensity for thinking of himself as the *Übermensch*, Miller is left with an ordinary man who makes an extraordinary choice, a hero of the minority, who stands alone as the strongest man in the world without sacrificing his humanity. For Miller, the moderated Dr. Stockmann is a transitional figure between the pathetically committed Joe Keller and Willy Loman and the idealistic John Proctor of *The Crucible*; between two men who clearly are wrong and one who clearly is right; between two men who attempt to exclude themselves from society's harsh judgment and a man whose personal commitment purposes a greater good; between two characters who can generate only pathos and a character who evokes the admiration and elevation of spirit of the tragically heroic common man.

Miller's hero in *The Crucible*, John Proctor, is a self-aware character who struggles to assert his identity and worth as an individual in the context of public terror and finds himself unexpectedly undergoing a hard reassessment of self. Though clearly a respected man in the community, Proctor's moral code derives from his own conscience, not from the Reverend Mr. Parris's fire-and-brimstone sermons. Proctor will miss attending church when he is angered by the minister's materialism and will plow his field on Sunday when the land needs working. When interrogated by the Reverend Mr. Hale as to his knowledge of the Commandments, he will forget one yet still not consider himself religiously remiss. Ironically, the Commandment that John's wife, Elizabeth, must remind him of is that concerning adultery, which has been his own sin. As the witchcraft trial intensifies, Proctor knows he will have to expose Abigail Williams as a whore in order to undermine the witch namer's credibility, but in doing so he will have to expose himself as well. And, finally, he will have to make the choice that others make with far greater ease: whether to confess himself a witch and be spared or insist on his innocence and be hanged. For Proctor, the ultimate value, a man's own conscience, prevails.

A prototype of Miller's contemporary hero, who is willing to lay down his life if need be to preserve his dignity, Proctor is a man of extraordinary moral courage. By contrast with those who too readily compromise and by parallel with Rebecca Nurse, who refuses to do so, Proctor becomes one of the few who survive the crucible, though he loses his life in doing so. A common man capable of uncommon moral strength, Proctor endorses values his neighbors fearfully deny. Though he softens on the day of his execution, not only confessing to witchcraft but signing a document of confession as well, he will not name names, and, finally, he will not permit the confession to be posted in public. Reneging, he agrees to death to preserve for his sons the honor of his name.

For Proctor, a name is a man's public self; to bring dishonor to his name is to bring social death to himself and his sons. As he fights to preserve the respect for the integrity of the individual, he frequently refers to the symbolic importance of names. In opposing the beginnings of the witch-hunt, he rebukes one of the primary advocates of the investigation, Thomas Putnam, pressuring Parris to follow Putnam's lead: "You cannot command Mr. Parris. We vote by name in this society, not by acreage."[4] When he confesses to lechery, he tells Danforth, "I have made a bell of my honor! I have rung the doom of my good name." To explain why his wife lies to protect him from the guilt of lechery, he explains, "She only thought to save my name!" When he is torn between saving his family by confessing to witchcraft and preserving the integrity of his name, his public self, he is caught in a dilemma. In confessing, he avoids seeing the others who refuse to confess because "they think to go like saints. I like not to spoil their names." In refusing, at first, to sign a written confession to be publicly displayed, he cries out, "I have confessed myself! Is there no good penitence but it be public? God does not need my name nailed upon the church! God sees my name; God knows how black my sins are! It is enough!" Finally, in refusing, he calls out, as Miller's stage direction has it, "with a cry of his whole soul": "Because it is my name! Because I cannot have another in my life! Because I lie and sign myself to lies! Because I am not worth the dust on the feet of them that hang! How may I live without my name? I have given you my soul; leave me my name!"

Others in the community who do not possess the sense of identity one's name provides are persuaded by the court that confession offers the only possibility of redemption. Not only do they admit to trafficking with the devil, but they name others as well. Parris's Barbados slave, Tituba, begins the naming when she herself is questioned and accused. At Mary Putnam's urging, Tituba had gone into the forest with a number of girls and, through her native magic, attempted to conjure Goody Putnam's dead babies, all seven of whom had died at birth. Tituba's imagination becomes especially active when, threatened with hanging, she hears Parris and Hale, the imported authority on demonology, tell her she is an agent of God, who will help in cleansing the village. Her example prompts Abigail to plead for the light of God and to add names to the list Tituba has begun. Parris's daughter, Betty, who has been in a trance—or feigning a trance—since her father came upon the dancing girls in the forest, joins the choral assignation of guilt to the respectable women and men of Salem. The hysterical litany of names that closes the first act and resonates throughout the trial is a terrifying incrimination of the New England theocracy that murdered in the name of God.

Abigail, who had once worked in the home of John and Elizabeth Proctor and to whom Proctor's lust had yielded, becomes the sustaining power behind the continuing obsession with witch-hunting that begins in the spring of 1692 and continues through the summer and the fall. A "strikingly beautiful girl, an orphan, with an endless capacity for dissembling," Abigail originally acts out of self-protection, as so many others in the community will do later. A shrewd opportunist, she turns her own violation of Salem law into an occasion for naming those for whom she has little liking and, in so doing, transforms herself into a local heroine. As a participant in Tituba's forest ceremony, Abigail drank blood, believing the ritual would curse Elizabeth Proctor, who, seven months earlier, suspecting her husband and Abigail, released the girl from their service. It is clear from a private conversation between Abigail and Proctor in act 1 that, though Proctor considers their affair over, Abigail still longs for him.

As Abigail takes center stage in the witchcraft hearings, John understands that she wants to dance with him on his wife's grave and that to do so she will orchestrate the unconscionable finger pointing that condemns to death a congeries of God-fearing citizens and forces innocent women to their knees in confession. Ready to believe Abigail and her teenage followers, the court indicts and summarily tries everyone the girls name, including Proctor's wife. But Elizabeth, whose goodness remains constant, will not confess; she is, ironically, spared death for a year so the unborn child she carries may be born.

Perhaps uncomfortable with his portrayal of Abigail as so unrelenting and unconscionable a young woman, Miller created a curious addition in an alternate version, moderating her vindictiveness, paralleling her commitment with that of the court officials, and alluding to the purgative process of the crucible. In this scene (2.2), which takes place in the forest, Abigail appears as a maddened religious fanatic whose mission is to expose the demons around her. She attributes her vision and zeal to Proctor, to whom she explains:

Why, you taught me goodness, therefore you are good. It were a fire you walked me through, and all my ignorance was burned away. It were a fire, John, we lay in fire. And from that night no woman dare call me wicked anymore but I knew my answer. I used to weep for my sins when the wind lifted up my skirts; and blushed for shame because some old Rebecca called me loose. And then you burned my ignorance away. As bare as some December tree I saw them all—walking like saints to church, running to feed the sick, and hypocrites in their hearts! And God gave me strength to call them liars, and God made men to listen to me, and by God I will scrub the world clean for love of Him! Oh, John, I will make you such a wife when the world is white again![5]

John, of course, has no intention in either version of marrying Abigail. When Elizabeth suspected a relationship between her husband and Abigail, he was overwhelmed by guilt and confessed the truth. Though he has had difficulty enduring Elizabeth's continuing judgment and the coldness of personality that existed even before the transgression, John's experiences with Abigail and with the Salem court have only increased his awareness of Elizabeth's goodness. When John humbles himself before the court, confessing to lechery in hopes that Abigail's exposure as a whore will end the readiness to believe her accusations, the court calls the honest Elizabeth from her cell for confirmation of John's claim. But if John was willing to sacrifice himself for his wife, Elizabeth is willing to sacrifice herself for her husband's good name. Publicly lying, she denies that her husband is a lecher.

The abiding goodness and respect that characterizes the relationship between John and Elizabeth expresses itself most forcefully in the final act, when John seeks Elizabeth's counsel. If John confesses, he will be saved; if he does not, he will hang that day. "What would you have me do?" he asks his wife, but she will not judge him: "As you will, I would have it." During the interview, Elizabeth tells her husband of Rebecca Nurse's imminent hanging and Giles Corey's pressing to death with stones, because he would not plead. She admits she wants him living, but she reminds him it is his soul, not hers. And she acknowledges her own sin in not knowing how to "say" her love. John cannot yield to dishonest confession; though it means he will hang, he tears up the document he has signed.

The Crucible is patterned in a detailed and accurate manner upon the historical records of the Salem witchcraft trials of 1692.[6] As a consequence of the fanaticism that characterized those trials, nineteen women and men and two dogs were hanged, one man was pressed to death for refusing to plead, and 150 were imprisoned; they were awaiting trial when a Boston court finally declared the evidence insufficient to warrant the death sentence. Communal participation in the witch-hunts was in response to the testimony of a group of girls and young women, aged nine to twenty, who fainted and cried out in hysteria as they named their prey. In "A Note on the Historical Accuracy of This Play," Miller observes that the fates of the characters in *The Crucible* coincide with those of their historical counterparts. In order to shape the historical material to suit his dramatic purpose, however, he made a number of minor alterations, at times representing several characters as one or two, as with the court officials, Hathorne and Danforth; reducing the number of girls involved in the witch naming; and, to make credible the invented relationship between Abigail Williams and John Proctor, turning a preadolescent girl into a seventeen-year-old.

Miller speaks as well of the historical characters and circumstances in Salem through a lengthy narrative beginning act 1 and through interruptive narrations throughout that act. The historical Parris, a fatherless widower with little understanding of or love for children, "cut a villainous path," apparently the consequence of a persecution complex. Thomas Putnam, son of the richest man in Salem, sought restitution for the village's rejection of his candidate for minister and contested his father's will when it favored his younger brother; Putnam's name appeared on a number of historical documents, characterizing him as an embittered, vindictive man. Francis Nurse was a frequent arbitrator in Salem, a man apparently capable of impartial judgment; he was, however, involved in a land dispute with his neighbors, including Putnam, and in the campaign for the ministerial candidate in opposition to Putnam's. It was Putnam who initiated the document accusing the highly respected Rebecca Nurse, Francis's wife, of witchcraft, and Putnam's young daughter who pointed hysterically and accusingly at the old woman at the hearing. Giles Corey, a man in his eighties at the time of the hearings, was the village misfit; careless of public opinion and casual about religion, he was the first to be suspected when a cow was missing or a fire blazed. And John Proctor, a farmer, was "the kind of man—powerful of body, even-tempered, and not easily led—who cannot refuse support to partisans without drawing their deepest resentment. In Proctor's presence a fool felt his foolishness instantly—and a Proctor is always marked for calumny therefore." But none of the personal animosities and motives of those involved in the purge at Salem seemed to be the concern of the court, which pursued its cause with a dedication and a zeal that

repeatedly endorsed Salem's heritage of "self-denial," "purposeful-
ness," "suspicion of all vain pursuits," and "hard-handed justice."
    Miller knew his dramatization of the Salem trials portrayed
society at its tyrannical worst, polarizing good and evil so that, for
his audience, those who opted to save their lives were clearly moral
cowards and those who hanged were heroes. Abigail, absent the
idealism she expressed in the forest, was unquestionably a fraud,
whose missionary zeal, though in tune with the genuine zeal of the
court, was unconscionable. And the court's officials as well, guardians of a misguided society's propensity for purity, carried out their
grim task with an energy and a dedication that a contemporary
audience could only associate with animated evil. Danforth and
Hathorne, who presided over the court, and the early Hale possessed and perpetuated a simplistic mentality that functioned in
polarities and in the assurance of right.
    Though such insistence upon absolute evil diminishes the com-
plexity of moral decision, Miller, in reflecting on *The Crucible*, was
sorry he did not emphasize the polarities even more:

I think now, almost four years after the writing of it, that I was wrong in
mitigating the evil of this man [Danforth] and the judges he represents.
Instead, I would perfect his evil to its utmost and make an open issue, a
thematic consideration of it in the play. I believe now, as I did not conceive
then, that there are people dedicated to evil in the world; that without their
perverse example we should not know the good. (*CP*, p. 43)

    The occasion for Miller's writing of *The Crucible* was clearly
the specter of McCarthyism that possessed America at the time. In
1950, Senator Joseph McCarthy of Wisconsin publicly charged that
205 communists had infiltrated the state department. Though he
could not name a single card-carrying communist, McCarthy trans-
formed his strident voice into a national mania. Before he was
censured in late 1954 by his own Senate colleagues, he had assas-
sinated the characters and ruined the professional lives of a host of
Americans, whom he accused of having communist sympathies.
The zealous guardian of the public good led a vulnerable country
through one of the darkest chapters in its history.
    The analogy between the McCarthy communist hunt and the
Salem witch-hunt was clearly fundamental to Miller's dramatic

strategy. But despite the effectiveness of the strategy—not to mention the artistic courage such a political action endorsed—Eric Bentley saw the analogy as erroneous; writing in 1953, he noted that, unlike witchcraft, "communism is not . . . merely a chimera."[7] Indeed, no one knew this better than Miller, who not only made the same acknowledgment in his narrative in the play but who was himself called before the House Committee on Un-American Activities three years after the opening of *The Crucible*. Facing an investigative process similar to that in Salem, Miller, unlike many of his contemporaries, survived professionally, escaping involvement in the ritualistic terror of exposing names of so-called communist subversives.[8]

In the introduction to *Collected Plays*, Miller observed that the climate in this country immediately preceding McCarthyism was one of a "new religiosity," an "official piety" that created new sins monthly and "above all horrors . . . accepted the notion that conscience was no longer a private matter but one of state administration" (*CP*, p. 40). But his attraction to the Salem witchcraft trials preceded his writing of *The Crucible* by some years. More than the specific, contemporary political madness, Miller saw in the Salem witch-hunts a model of the subtle but devastating usurpation of political purity by the religious mentality. The Salem affair was emblematic of a presiding communal and personal guilt that the hysteria did not create but unleashed. A repressive society, Salem endorsed an austere life of self-denial that was enforced by communally created laws dedicated to preserving order and public authority.

But individual, personal guilt figured strongly in Miller's drama as well. If the historical Salem court ignored personal animosity, Miller's play repeatedly suggests impure motives, creating quarrels between Proctor and Parris over whether the minister's firewood should be included in his salary and between Proctor and Putnam over a piece of land, creating jealousy on the part of Abigail over Elizabeth and suspicion on the part of Elizabeth over her husband and Abigail. Abigail's animosity toward Elizabeth is a clear example of a vindictiveness that Abigail has been unable, for seven months, to express any more effectively than in her response to Parris's early query. There she imputed hatred and bitterness to Abigail, defending her own good name and calling Goody Proctor a "gossiping liar." Through Tituba's confession, Miller more subtly suggests the extent to which repressed desire found a forum in the Salem witch-hunts. When forced to admit her relationship with the devil, Tituba immediately charges the devil with discrediting Parris, coaxing her into killing him, just as, the confession implies, Tituba might have liked to have done.

As Miller points out, the witch-hunt was "a long overdue op-portunity for everyone so inclined to express publicly his guilt and sins, under the cover of accusations against the victims" (CP, p. 229). For those who confessed to trafficking with the devil, the witchcraft hearings provided both an opportunity to articulate guilt in a specific form and a forum for expression. In a society that nurtures through its repressiveness an abiding sense of personal guilt, there is freedom in falling to one's knees and agreeing to the most heinous of sins, face-to-face communion with evil. It is not difficult to imagine members of the Salem community secretly hop-ing their names would be the next to be called, for in such a climate people not only want others to be guilty, they want their own guilt recognized as well, even as they fear the consequence.

Like Ibsen, Miller has always been interested in the question of guilt; in *All My Sons*, he examined the toxic consequences of hid-den culpability on the part of the head of a family. But Joe Keller is guilty of a specific crime of commission; for other Miller charac-ters, including many in *The Crucible*, guilt is a less specific quality of mind. When urged into communal expression by a public forum, such guilt acquires enormous power. Dennis Welland rightly ob-serves that "in the life of a society evil is occasioned less by deliber-ate villainy than by the abnegation of personal responsibility," by the failure of the individual to assert and define his sense of self-worth.[9] Such guilt, which Miller will repeatedly acknowledge and examine in his subsequent work, greatly inhibits that defense.

5

A View from the Bridge

In the introduction to *Collected Plays*, Miller speaks of his disappointment in discovering that none of the reviewers of *The Crucible*, regardless of their assessment, identified the play as a drama about "the handing over of conscience to another . . . and the realization that with conscience goes the person, the soul immortal, and the 'name.'"[1] It became important to him, therefore, "to separate, openly and without concealment, the action of the next play, *A View from the Bridge*, from its generalized significance," which, for Miller, was

the awesomeness of a passion which, despite its contradicting the self-interest of the individual it inhabits, despite every kind of warning, despite even its destruction of the moral beliefs of the individual, proceeds to magnify its power over him until it destroys him. (*CP*, p. 48)

Miller had heard of Eddie Carbone's prototype years earlier, and the story kept insisting on dramatic form. For Miller, however, a drama capable of accommodating the story would have to preserve a series of actions he regarded as incapable of interpretation, while at the same time expressing his sense of the meaning those actions held for him. Moreover, it would have to allow an audience to interpret the event for itself. Miller's means of accomplishing all three was the engaged narrator.

Alfieri, Eddie's lawyer, begins and ends *A View from the Bridge* with direct addresses to the audience and punctuates its action with patches of storytelling, comments on his own reactions, and judgments. Like Miller, who was haunted by the story of Eddie's prototype, Alfieri cannot dismiss the longshoreman from his mind. He thinks often of Eddie and of how, even as he lived through the events with him, he felt both detached and involved. Capable of predicting with certainty the destructive end of Eddie's course, he at the same time was powerless to prevent it. Though no determinist, Alfieri knew that when Eddie's stubborn commitment came face to face with the moral laws of the Brooklyn community in which he lived, the emanating power would have the force of ancient gods. As narrator, Alfieri becomes less a teller of the tale than a choric measure of what is enduringly human, a judge of the destructive choices that Eddie feels obliged to make when conflicting values claim him. Alfieri watches with a sense of his own impotence as Eddie grapples with some of the same questions Joe Keller, Willy Loman, and John Proctor faced.

The question of which laws require a man's primary allegiance becomes central — and lethal — for Eddie Carbone, who cannot reconcile the social laws and the moral laws that claim him. As a United States citizen, Eddie is bound by the law of his nation, including an immigration law in which he does not believe. But as a member of the Sicilian community of the Red Hook section of Brooklyn, he has a commitment to unwritten subcultural law, which prescribes communal conduct — and protects illegal immigrants. As head of a family, Eddie endorses traditional familial values, particularly strong among Sicilians, that make his word domestic law. But as a member of the human community, Eddie respects a natural law that refuses even to allow him to admit that he is sexually attracted to his niece.

The simultaneous demands of these several laws so confuse Eddie that he commits what the community holds as the most heinous of crimes, invoking a law for which he himself has little regard in order to do so. Unable to prevent his niece, Catherine, from marrying Rodolpho, an illegal immigrant living in his own home, Eddie turns informer, an act resulting in the arrest of Rodolpho, his brother Marco, and two others. From a position of respect within the community, earned in part through his own hospitality to "submarines," Eddie tumbles to a position of contempt. As Eddie's neighbors and his fellow longshoremen scorn him, he defends himself by denying his guilt and by accusing his accuser: Marco is "crazy! I give them the blankets off my bed. Six months I kept them like my own brothers!" Eddie knows he has betrayed his community's values, yet he is unwilling to sacrifice his name. Even after he has violated the community code of honor, Eddie argues in terms of that code, insisting upon his innocence on the strength of the six months in which he housed the two men and demanding a form of justice that has been culturally endorsed for centuries.

Eddie will have his Sicilian justice, but it will prove him wrong. When Marco turns to Alfieri for counsel, he learns why "in Sicily . . . the law has not been a friendly idea since the Greeks were beaten." The legal system provides no means for punishing Eddie's crime. Hence Marco turns to Sicilian law, defending his honor in the street even as the misguided Eddie defends his own. As the instrument of Eddie's death, Marco symbolically affirms a moral law that Alfieri's law ignores.

Communal law condemns Eddie to shame and to death, but the impulse for violating that law has little to do with the conflict between it and federal law. Eddie and his family have always endorsed subcultural law; he and his wife, Beatrice, even tell Catherine what happened to Vinny Bolzano, a fourteen-year-old who informed on an uncle staying in his home:

Oh, it was terrible. He had five brothers and the old father. And they grabbed him in the kitchen and pulled him down the stairs—three flights his head was bouncin' like a coconut. And they spit on him in the street, his own father and his brothers. The whole neighborhood was cryin'. (*CP*, p. 389)

Eddie's explanation of the significance of the betrayal is a harshly ironic comment on his own fate: "Just remember, kid, you can quicker get back a million dollars that was stole than a word that you gave away." Eddie gives that word away, though, informing the authorities of the illegal immigrants, not because his conscience has moved away from that of the Red Hook community but because he can see no other way to prevent the marriage of his niece to Rodolpho.

Eddie has brought up the orphaned Catherine as his daughter. He is fond of the young woman and gets upset when Catherine wears spike-heel shoes, when she "walks wavy" in her new short skirt, and when she proposes to take a secretarial job on the docks.

Like any father who has difficulty permitting his daughter passage from girlhood to womanhood, Eddie imposes restrictions on the seventeen-year-old that keep her close to home. But when Rodolpho comes to live with them, the young man's interest in Catherine prompts a passionate, antagonistic response from Eddie that clearly exceeds his fatherly role.

Rodolpho is not the kind of man Eddie wants for Catherine—if indeed he wants anyone at all. Not only does he not ask permission of Eddie to take Catherine to the movies, he spends all of his first paycheck on a sports jacket and pointy shoes. Suspicious that Rodolpho wants to marry Catherine just to obtain citizenship, Eddie complains bitterly—and jealously—to Alfieri of his own sacrifice and Rodolpho's ingratitude. But Eddie objects to Rodolpho on other grounds as well: unlike the dark, swarthy Italians of the longshore community, Rodolpho is platinum blond; he cooks and sews and sings "Paper Doll" on the docks in a tenor voice. As Eddie watches the relationship between his niece and Rodolpho develop, he keeps insisting the "guy ain't right." When he decides, finally, that the man is homosexual, he has legitimate cause to prevent, at all costs, the dishonorable marriage.

Eddie does not admit what others see: that he is attracted to his niece in a way that has little to do with culturally endorsed father-daughter love. Alfieri's response to Eddie's distress over Rodolpho indicates the lawyer's awareness of what Eddie will not admit and may not even recognize: that he has too much love for his niece. Eddie cannot comprehend Alfieri's meaning and moves to punish Rodolpho with the law. Ironically, he does not prevent the marriage, but, in breaking faith with his family and the community, he becomes an object of scorn. Alfieri had warned him he would be friendless and Eddie knew he was right, but he convinced himself that protecting Catherine from the manufactured dishonor of a marriage to Rodolpho was more important than honoring the communal law that protects Rodolpho. Driven by a passion he does not understand, Eddie makes the decision that assures the destruction Alfieri saw from the start.

Eddie's refusal to accept his own vulnerability releases an insuperable power that, though of human origin, finally exceeds the human. With the inexorability of Greek tragedy, the play carries

Eddie to his destruction, victim of an inevitability he himself creates. But Eddie's unwillingness to compromise reminds Alfieri of a finer value than most people need, something "perversely pure."

In the earlier one-act version of *A View from the Bridge*, Miller was especially concerned with creating a sense of deliberateness and direction. Miller described the one-act version as a "hard, telegraphic, unadorned drama. Nothing was permitted which did not advance the progress of Eddie's catastrophe in a most direct way."[2] After he saw the play in production several times, however, Miller's attitude toward Eddie changed. His central character became less a "phenomenon, a rather awesome fact of existence" than a man who, however much one might dislike him, possesses "the wondrous and humane fact that he too can be driven to what in the last analysis is a sacrifice of himself for his conception, however misguided, of right, dignity, and justice" (*CP*, p. 51). In writing the two-act version, Miller explored the causes behind Eddie's actions. Once his attitude toward Eddie changed, he could approach Beatrice and Catherine in a different context. No longer "muted counterpoints to the march of Eddie's career," they become "involved forces pressing him forward or holding him back and eventually forming, in part, the nature of his disaster" (*CP*, p. 51).

In the two-act version, Miller develops the conflict between Beatrice and Eddie that is only mentioned in the original. In the one-act play, Eddie explains his concern for Catherine by saying, "I'm responsible for her," to which his wife replies, "I just wish once in a while you'd be responsible for me, you know that?"[3] Beatrice's statement implies that Eddie is not fulfilling his role as a husband, but Miller does not develop the issue until the two-act play. Here Beatrice is a far more articulate and passionate woman than her counterpart in the original, and the charges of sexual neglect she makes against Eddie are more explicit. Moreover, her probing suggests the correlation between Eddie's brooding concern for Catherine and his alienation from Beatrice. In the two-act play, Beatrice realizes what both Catherine and Eddie are unable to recognize about themselves: that they are on the edge of incest.

In the final scene of the one-act play, Eddie openly expresses his love for Catherine, kissing her on the lips, saying *"like a lover, out of his madness*: It's me, ain't it?" When Marco stabs him, he crawls a yard to Catherine to die at her feet; "puzzled, questioning, betrayed," he asks, "Catherine—why—?"⁴ In the two-act play, Catherine tells Eddie, "I never meant to do nothing bad to you":

EDDIE: Then why—Oh, B.!
BEATRICE: Yes, yes!
EDDIE: My B.! (CP, p. 439)

Eddie's dying words affirm his love for his wife and repudiate his incestuous desire for his niece.

The second version of the play is at once more subtle in presenting Eddie's subliminal sexuality and more assured in its suggestion of its influence. In the original, Catherine is openly resentful of Eddie's advice and of his authority over her. Her resentment springs from Eddie's attempts to restrain her and to discourage the signs that she is no longer a child but a woman. When, for example, Eddie sees Catherine's high-heel shoes, he immediately criticizes her for wearing them. When Catherine rejoins that she is only trying them out, he replies: "When I'm home I'm not in the movies, / I don't wanna see young girls / Walking around in spike-heel shoes."⁵

Catherine's resentment is more forcefully dramatized in the one-act version, and Eddie's protectiveness, his love, and his hostility concerning his niece are more directly expressed. In an early scene, Eddie tells Catherine: "You're the Madonna type. That's why you shouldn't be flashy, Kate. For you it ain't beautiful. You're more the Madonna type. And anyway, it ain't nice in an office. They don't go for that in an office."⁶ Catherine, in the one-act version, does not respond. Two brief scenes later, when Eddie complains that Rodolpho has "got her rollin'; you see the way she looks at him? The house could burn down she wouldn't know,"⁷ Beatrice tells him to let Catherine be "somebody else's Madonna now."⁸ In the two-act version, Eddie's criticism of her new shoes and Catherine's reaction are more suggestive of the tenderness between them and of the undertones of sexuality. In this version, Catherine is more dependent upon Eddie, more moved by his protests, more in conflict over what she would like to do and what Eddie would have her do.

In revising the play, Miller clearly rethought his original principle of presenting Eddie's story as a "hard outline of a human dilemma" (*CP*, p. 50) and chose to explore the emotional conflict more deeply. But in so doing, Miller moved the play closer to the realistic mode, emphasizing the passion that he admitted was central not only to drama but to this particular play as well. A comment on the set in the earlier version suggests an emphasis on the play's non-realistic quality as a means of endorsing the urgency of the action and of seeing Eddie not as an individual but as part of a continuum of human experience present both in contemporary Brooklyn and in ancient Italy. That stage direction expresses Miller's intention "to make concrete the ancient element of this tale through the unmitigated forms of the commonest life of the big-city present, the one playing against the other to form a new world on the stage."[9]

In "On Social Plays," Miller speaks of his feeling that he had heard Eddie's story before: "After a time I thought that it must be some re-enactment of a Greek myth which was ringing a long-buried bell in my own subconscious mind."[10] Miller suggests this nagging sense of the mythical nature of the story through Alfieri's choric role. With the omniscience of a Greek chorus and the detachment of one most fully involved as observer, Alfieri sees what Eddie himself cannot see, foresees the consequences of Eddie's actions, offers advice he knows will not be received, and comments afterwards on Eddie's destruction. In the one-act play, Alfieri's choric role is especially strong, Miller having created most of his lines in verse. In the two-act play, Alfieri's function remains choric, but his idiom is colloquial prose, shifting the play's balance toward realism.

The revised play was performed in London in 1956, where Peter Brook's staging contributed further to its realism. Brook introduced details of the Italian-American neighborhood and added more walk-on characters, strengthening the concept of community and more solidly establishing the context for Eddie's betrayal. The next year, Brook brought the play to Paris, with two modifications: an acknowledgment in the play of Catherine's awareness of Eddie's sexual attraction to her (added to satisfy what Brook and Miller assessed as a more sexually sophisticated audience) and a change in

Eddie's death scene. Responding to some dissatisfaction that it was Marco who killed Eddie, Miller handed the knife over not to Rodolpho but to Eddie himself, who committed suicide.[11]

It was the 1956 play, however, that became the standard and that Miller selected for *Collected Plays*. That play has enjoyed a number of revivals, including a long run in 1965 off-Broadway, starring first Robert Duvall and then Robert Castellano, and a stellar-cast production on Broadway in 1983, with Tony LoBianco. Responses to the recent production were predictably mixed, with John Simon, still measuring the play against a classical conception of tragedy, dismissing it as "pretentious melodrama" and Frank Rich calling it a "vivid, crackling, idiomatic psychosexual horror tale": LoBianco as Eddie is "such a dynamic and enveloping force that the audience has no chance to even think of questioning the play until well after it's over." Clive Barnes's observation, though, may best identify that quality of Miller's writing that will assure the continuing attraction of *A View from the Bridge*:

Critics cavil at Miller—unhappily I do myself—but they never stop him. His plays hit a nerve accurately but critics tend to forget the unerring aim and only concentrate on the clumsy weapon. This is Miller's conundrum—he writes so cheaply, yet his dramatic effects are priceless.[12]

6

❖❖

A Memory of
Two Mondays

In the introduction to *Collected Plays*, Miller speaks of the reception of *A View from the Bridge* in New York, noting that while the two-act version, performed in London, was a better play, it was "not that much better." The New York production failed, he felt, at least in part because it shared the evening with *A Memory of Two Mondays*, which was "dismissed so thoroughly that in one of the reviews, and one of the most important, it was not even mentioned as having been played":

By the time *A View from the Bridge* came on, I suppose the critics were certain that they were witnessing an aberration, for there had been no suggestion of any theatrical authority in the first play's performance. It was too much to hope that the second play could retrieve what had been so completely dissipated by the first.[1]

Those reviewers who did mention *A Memory of Two Mondays* were hardly charitable. Richard Hayes, writing for *Commonweal*, called the play "uninterruptedly bad." *Time* saw it as "a pat, shapeless picture of life in a warehouse during the Depression." And Brooks Atkinson of the *New York Times* dismissed the play as a "pedestrian chronicle of workaday life in a Manhattan warehouse," refusing to say more about that half of the double bill.[2] Still, in the introduction to *Collected Plays*, Miller claims that *A Memory of Two Mondays* has more of his affection than any of the others: "Nothing in this book was written with greater love, and for myself I love nothing printed here better than this play" (*CP*, p. 49).

Miller speaks of the piece as one that helped him define the value of hope. His own youthful experience parallels that of Bert, who, until he has enough money saved for college, is working in an auto-parts warehouse in New York, among people who will spend their lives in the daily tedium of receiving, filling, and shipping. When Bert saves enough money, he leaves, expecting some gesture from his co-workers, but they hardly notice his departure.

Miller describes the piece as a "pathetic comedy," depicting a narrow and prescriptive life. The world of Miller's play suggests that of Beckett's *Waiting for Godot*, which was to appear on the New York stage within a year. For Didi and Gogo, the roadside under the tree is the circumscribed world of their existence; they return to it each day to fill the space of time with activity that takes them nowhere but that assures them they exist. Miller's play world is a warehouse of endless receiving and shipping, of tedium, of waiting, and of returning the next day to live through the routine again. Vivien Mercier once described *Waiting for Godot* as "a play in which nothing happens, twice."[3] The same may be said of *A Memory of Two Mondays*, set first on a Monday in summer and, later, on a Monday in winter. On both days, the same characters are at work, their activity unchanged. Mr. Eagle, unlike Godot, does appear, several times, to inspect and to endorse their work and their existence.

But in Miller's play, Bert breaks away, conscious of the deadening force of habit and saddened by the indifference with which his departure is met. As much as Beckett's play, Miller's renders a portrait of the contemporary human being, suffering from a paralysis that comes from yielding to the insistent tedium of daily activity that seems to be the only measure of worth. As Bert observes, "There's something so terrible here! / . . . It's like the subway; / Every day I see the same people getting on / and the same people getting off, / And all that happens is that they get older. God!"

But Miller's play, like Beckett's, also affirms the value of community. Miller describes his play as "a search for some fundamental fiat, not moral in itself but ultimately so, which keeps a certain order among us."[4] *A Memory of Two Mondays* evokes a sense of sympathy for others, a sense of a common fate.

On the first Monday of the two, warehouse workers take their places at a few minutes before nine, readying themselves for their shift in the shipping room, where they will spend the day taking orders off the hook, selecting the parts from the bins, and setting the merchandise on the table, where Kenneth packages and address-es the parts. Bert enters first, carrying his lunch, a copy of *War and Peace*, and the *New York Times*, wanting to get in some reading before the workday begins. He chats with Raymond, the manager, about local events, his references to Hitler setting the time in 1933. This is America between the wars, people between birth and death, toiling to pass the hours in the space between.

One by one the employees report for work: Raymond, in his forties, the manager; Agnes, later forties, unmarried, always with a laugh; Patricia, twenty-three, pretty, talking about her dates; Gus, sixty-eight, barrel-bellied and bald, coming off a weekend binge with Jim, in his seventies, who fought the Indians in his youth; Kenneth, twenty-six, an Irishman who recites poetry and complains of the dust; Larry, thirty-nine, father of triplets, who buys himself a new car; Frank, in his thirties, truck driver and womanizer; Jerry and Willy, both twenty-three, slick dressers, Jerry with a black eye; and Tom, in his late forties, a drunk. Miller draws broad pencil outlines of his characters that he does not need to fill in. They might as readily be any of the millions in the American work force—or anywhere else—concerned with the community within their micro-cosm but with little else.

But the characters are sketchy too because this is a memory play, filtered through the perceptions of Bert, who, as a temporary employee, remains somewhat on the outside. No longer among these people, Bert remembers impressionistically the incessant rou-tine of day after day in the warehouse, and he remembers with clarity isolated moments in their communal and private lives: Gus calling home after a weekend on the town to explain to a deaf wife that he is all right; Gus receiving the call from a neighbor who tells him his Lilly has died. Tom, coming in drunk the day Mr. Eagle is due, being propped up at a table, pencil in hand, Bert leaning over him staging conversation; Gus protecting Tom from being fired, offering his own job as testament to his faith in Tom; Jim talking about fighting the Indians; Kenneth reciting poetry and objecting to the dust; Larry buying an Auburn when he could ill afford it be-cause he liked the valves; Larry directing Bert down corridors of auto parts to an obsolete part; Agnes, laughing or crying, refusing Gus's invitation to Atlantic City; Patricia talking about her dates. And, in between, there is the tedium, the monotonous motion required to fill the pile of orders assigned them for the day. If the first Monday creates the tone for life in an auto warehouse—or anywhere—the second returns to those same people, registering both continuity and change. Tom has given up drinking, but Henry has begun. Tom realized he had made it when at the Christmas party he mixed drinks for three hours but never touched one himself. Kenneth spends much of his time drunk, denying his addiction, and he is unable now to remember poems. Earlier, Kenneth, enlisting Bert's help, washes all the windows, providing them all with a view of the outside world. He swipes a rag across a window, and all the windows instantly become clean, the stage lit in a flood of sunshine. Peering out, he delights in the lovely backyard he sees. But by the second Monday, the scene has changed to a bevy of naked women occupying a whorehouse across the way. Angry at the excitement of Jerry and Willy, who keep crowding around his table so they can see the view, Kenneth explodes: "Is that all yiz know of the world—filthy women and dirty jokes and the ignorance drippin' off your faces?" But Kenneth's own desire to know the world has itself diminished. Stuck in the auto warehouse forty hours a week, he talks nostalgically about a civil service job but shows no potential for making the change. Yielding to the deadening habit of his job, he prefers drink to poetry, unconsciousness to the exhilaration of life. This is year one in the warehouse for Kenneth, but it has already claimed his soul.

If Kenneth opts for an anesthetic stupor, Gus awakens from a lethargy of twenty-two years, acquiring consciousness and the pain that accompanies it. In a curious way, Gus, as unlikely a candidate as any, replaces Kenneth as poet laureate of the play. At sixty-eight, Gus loses weekends to drink, wears smelly long underwear, and looks like King Kong. But there is something finer in Gus, who defends his friend Tom when the younger man's job is at risk and who is crushed by the death of the woman he liked a lot, his Lilly. Gus does his job devotedly, counseling others on matters that are often none of his business, yet even on the first Monday he is heard to complain. Though he spends weekends attempting to obliterate consciousness, it creeps back on Monday morning to remind him of what he does not want to know. When Kenneth comments to Larry, "Oh, there must be a terrible lot of Monday mornings in sixteen years. And no philosophical idea at all, y'know, to pass the time?", Gus immediately interrupts: "When you gonna shut up?"

On the second Monday, Gus appears, bottle in hand, taking inventory of his life. He worked at the warehouse for twenty-two years, and, when his wife died, she was home alone. He is ready for rebellion. Gus speaks of how he measures his warehouse time, turning a succession of automobiles from the Winston six to the Cleveland car, into a poetic summary of his life. Though it is only nine-thirty, Gus leaves the warehouse, dressed in his cemetery visiting clothes, his pockets full of his insurance money, and never returns. But Jim, who was with him, reports: they hit all the bars on Third Avenue, from the bottom to Fourteenth Street, picked up some girls, then hailed three cabs, the third to follow in case either of the other two got a flat. When the cabs stopped at a light, Jim checked on Gus; he was dead in the cab. After twenty-two years, Gus opts for out, but leaving the warehouse means death.

Of the dozen workers, only Bert leaves, having taken the job in the first place as a temporary one. *War and Peace* read, money in the bank, Bert spends his last Monday at the warehouse, among people he knows he will never forget. Yet Bert knows too that in a month or two they will forget his name and confuse him with other eighteen-year-olds who worked there. He looks for their acknowledgment that he has touched them, but he finds only token goodbyes. The daily routine prevails, uninterrupted by Bert's parting; they take orders from the hook, gather up the goods, place them on the table for Kenneth to wrap.

But Kenneth, seeing Bert is gone, experiences once again the poetry of life, if only vicariously. His farewell to Bert is from the Irish poet Thomas Moore, who speaks of the Minstrel Boy gone to war:

> " . . . in the ranks of death you will find him;
> His father's sword he has girded on,
> And his wild harp slung behind him." (*CP*, p. 376)

Though he himself has failed, Kenneth recognizes the potential in Bert and sings his heroic farewell. Bert, who could defend his reading of *War and Peace* only on instinct—"Well, it's—it's literature"—has the enthusiasm, the compassion, the devotion to find poetry in life. An unlessoned boy, Bert emerges from the warehouse with a purity the others have long relinquished and with a compassion for those he leaves behind.

Although the play is performed in the present, its title suggests that Bert has achieved some distance, both in time and in perception, and that now he understands. He understands that the warehouse of tedium and monotony crushes the life of the imagination, the spirit that invites some to poetry and that cleans the windows of the world. But he understands as well that in its place the warehouse workers have found a community, a devotion to their minor tasks and to each other that earns compassion and respect. Bert sees himself not only as a poet but as a privileged person, whose recording of his memory of two Mondays responds to a poetry of life present even in "a world in which things are endlessly sent and endlessly received."[4]

7

* *

After the Fall

When Miller returned to the legitimate stage in 1964 after an eight-year absence, he brought with him an unaltered preoccupation with culpability and guilt. *After the Fall*, which opened the Vivian Beaumont Theater's first season at Lincoln Center, and *Incident at Vichy*, which opened the following year's season,[1] both offer profiles of postlapsarian humanity, governed by the guilt of individual and collective failing. In a foreword to *After the Fall*, Miller speaks of Eve's tasting of the forbidden fruit as the end of paradise and innocence, the beginning of consciousness and choice. And he warns against "complicity with Cain," whose alternative was "to express without limit one's unbridled inner compulsion . . . and to plead unawareness as a virtue and a defense."[2] For Miller, the modern equivalent of the fall from paradise is the German concentration camp, after which there can be no innocence. Everyone, these plays suggest, bears the guilt, for everyone is either actively involved as oppressor or tacitly involved as observer or oppressed.

In *After the Fall*, a brick watchtower of a concentration camp looms over the action of the play, activated in several postwar scenes as a skeleton of the horror it recalls and serving as a physical context within which Quentin, the play's introspective protagonist, measures his domestic and professional responsibilities. Obsessed with trying to understand why he continually searches for hope despite repeated disappointment and why he still awakens each morning feeling the promise of the new day, Quentin is a man who has come to see life as a law case before an empty bench in a courtroom in which there is no judge and no verdict. His quest is to achieve a balance between acceptance and rejection of responsibility and guilt. The play is an odyssey of individual anguish, a "trial of a man by his own conscience, his own values, his own deeds."[3]

The form of *After the Fall* enables Miller to range freely between past and present and to explore Quentin's personal agony in
several contexts. The play's action, consisting of freely associated
but highly selected memories, takes place in Quentin's mind. Quentin speaks to a Listener, presumably seated just offstage, reviewing
major events of his life as each is dramatized on the gray landscape
of the set. Unlike *Death of a Salesman*, which clearly defines memory space and present space, here the boundaries between the present
and the past and among various events of the past fluidly shape the
space. All of the characters remain onstage throughout Quentin's
confessional, each activated in turn by the narrative. The Listener,
never identified, may be a psychoanalyst, a friend, a rabbi, God, or,
as Miller suggests, Quentin himself "turned at the edge of the abyss
to look at his experience, his nature and his time."[4]

The occasion for the interview with the Listener, which is a
monologue, is Quentin's return from Europe, where he met and fell
in love with Holga. It has been just fifteen months since the death of
his second wife, Maggie, fourteen months since he quit his position
at the law firm, and five months since his mother died. The year has
been one of defeats and reassessments, of emotional lows that
seemed unredeemable; but now, with Holga, the promise has returned. As Quentin begins his narrative, a character from upstage
steps forward to interrupt him. It is Felice, a client whose divorce he
handled, a woman who admired her attorney and with whom
Quentin would have liked to have made love. Quentin does not
understand why Felice appears, nor why Maggie's laughter sings
out from among the men upstage, but such seemingly random ap-
pearances dictate the play's structure and mirror Quentin's mental
associations. He wants to tell the story of Holga, to seek endorsement from the Listener, but Holga exists for him only within the
context of his other relationships, and each of those must, in turn,
pass through his mind. Hence the narrative yields to scenes of
Quentin's boyhood; of his father's bankruptcy and his mother's
death; of his friend, Lou, whose radical politics led him to suicide;
of his colleague, Mickey, who, called before the House Committee,
named names; of Felice, who will always bless him; of Elise, whose
bathrobe kept slipping off her shoulders; of Louise, his wife of ten
years; and of Maggie, the most haunting of his relationships, the

one life he must understand in relation to his own before he can justify Holga.

The possibility of self-knowledge and of hope that ends the two-hour session with the Listener is the consequence not of random storytelling but of Quentin's systematic examination of experience measured in terms of the Fall. As Miller noted in "Our Guilt for the World's Evil," "The first problem is . . . to discover our own relationship to evil, its reflection of ourselves."[5] Quentin's probing personal memories become excursions into "the nature of the human being himself," which, the play finally suggests, is "the only source of the violence which has come closer and closer to destroying the race."[6]

The Quentin who appears in the Listener's space is in a state of indecision, uncertain whether he can responsibly marry the woman he has met. She appears to offer him a hope that a survey of his life suggests should be an empty one, but he is besieged by self-doubt and fear. As Miller describes Quentin's dilemma, "He is faced, in short, with what Eve brought to Adam—the terrifying fact of choice."[7]

As the desperate man moves mentally through his past, it becomes clear that Quentin's recapitulation, like any historical process, is highly selective. The story he most wants to tell is Maggie's, for his relationship with her is the consummate tale of the failed innocence mirrored in every other memory to which Quentin's unconscious mind leads him. Present throughout the session, Maggie tugs at Quentin's memory several times during the first act but succeeds in occupying it only once, for his recollection of their first encounter. On that occasion, she ingenuously speaks of the man who walked off with her dog, which wasn't hers in the first place; of her search for a discount record store; of her efforts to discourage rude men; of her affair with the deceased judge, whose family would not admit her to his funeral; of her thick, inherited hair. As Maggie leaves, Quentin gives her cab money and counsel, wishing she could recognize her vulnerability. It will be four years before the two meet again, yet Maggie has inspired and refreshed Quentin. Though Louise misconstrues his confession—that "it would have been easy to make love to her"—its purity is intact: Quentin has been touched by uncommon innocence and trust: "she wasn't defending anything, upholding anything, or accusing—she was just *there*."⁸

His attraction to Maggie, which eventually leads to their marriage, the failure of their marriage, and her overdose of sleeping pills, becomes an expression of a temptation of Innocence, a desire to return to a world before the Fall. Through Maggie, Quentin comes to understand that innocence no longer exists but that the myth of Innocence impedes the quest: if Quentin is to be a self, he must obliterate all that obstructs him, including what he loves.

The process of dramatic articulation provides the means of destruction, for, as Quentin resurrects characters and situations from the past, giving them conscious shape, he destroys their unconscious hold on him. But individually exposed and collectively assembled, Quentin's episodic memories gradually cohere into a thematic and emotional whole: Maggie's is not the only story of false innocence, nor is anyone in Quentin's past—parents, friends, or lovers—without guilt. Midway into the first-act narrative, Quentin identifies his "final bafflement": "Is it altogether good to be not guilty for what another does?"

Felice, the first to appear in Quentin's memory, keeps insisting on goodness and a purity in which Quentin would like to believe. She tells him of how, as they were leaving Quentin's law office, her newly divorced husband suggested they make love one more time. Despite his own experience, Quentin assures her that hatred does not destroy love. To the Listener, though, he reproaches himself for his own stupidity. Quentin has become Felice's romantic ideal; she understands that it does not matter to him whether she has a big nose or a small one, so she goes ahead with her nose bobbing. Her refrain, the one line that Quentin repeatedly recalls, is "I will always bless you." Through Felice, he sees himself as a savior, a man of ultimate goodness, willingly taking on the burdens of others. It is a vision of which he must disabuse himself, but, as Felice leaves, he does a "stupid thing":

I don't understand it. There are two light fixtures on the wall of my hotel room. *Against his own disgust*, I noticed for the first time that they're . . . a curious distance apart. And I suddenly saw that if you stood be-

tween them—*He spreads out his arms*—you could reach out and rest your.
. . . (CP2, p. 137)

He recalls the sacrificial posture again in act 2, confessing now that

I didn't do it, but I wanted to. Like . . .
   He turns and spreads his arms in crucifixion.
. . . this!
   In disgust he lowers his arms.
. . . I don't know! Because she . . . *gave* me something! She . . . let me
change her! As though I—*Cries out*—felt something! *He almost laughs.*
What the hell am I trying to do, love *everybody*? (CP2, p. 202)

     Quentin's vision of universal love, expressed in the context of
the crucifixion, suggests his attraction to prelapsarian Innocence,
redeemed through Christ's sacrifice. But before his quest for an
understanding of love can materialize, he must discover that its
context is not prelapsarian but after the Fall.
     The image of Eve is embodied in Lou's wife, Elsie, the woman
whose robe kept slipping off her shoulders and who stood naked
before him in his bedroom. Quentin naively registers his shock at
the unspoken proposition of this contemporary, cultured Eve, who
tempts him to reenact the archetypal testing of the forbidden fruit:

I tell you I believed she didn't know she was naked! It's Eden! . . .
Well, she was *married*! How could a woman who can tell when the Buda-
pest String Quartet is playing off key, who refuses to wear silk stockings
because the Japanese have invaded Manchuria, whose husband—my
friend, a saintly professor of law—is editing my first appeal to the Supreme
Court on the grass outside that window—I could see the top of his head
past her tit, for God's sake! (CP2, pp. 149–50)

Quentin's moral indignation is a disguise for his reluctance to participate in the destruction of Innocence, the consequence of which is
responsibility and choice. Despite Elsie's shameless appeal, he still
wants to believe that trust, faith, goodness, and innocence define
human nature. But each encounter with a character from his past
urges him to reconsider.
     He recalls the moment when he told his father that his mother

had just died. They had been married for fifty years, and Quentin and his brother thought it would be like sawing off his arm, yet, a few months later, the old man registered to vote. He remembers the maternal voice of the woman who warned him not to play with matches and scorned his handwriting as monkey scrawl. He remembers her disappointment when the man she thought a hero became her husband and needed her to read the menu. But most poignantly he remembers the night he overheard his father confessing to his mother that he had lost everything, even her bonds, and that they were financially depleted. Hearing of his financial failure, she scorns her husband, calling him an idiot and reproaching herself in self-pity; to her young son, Quentin, she denies she ever said such a thing.

He remembers the day his colleague Mickey, called before the House Committee on Un-American Activities, decided to name names. Mickey was a man who was always astonished at Quentin's marital fidelity; he himself played around but made certain that each day he treated his wife as someone he was meeting for the first time. He discovered another dimension to fidelity when he resolved to tell the truth about his communist activities and, more importantly, to tell the truth about others. Colleagues turned their backs on him; Lou, the last to hear, saw Mickey's need to tell the truth as breaking faith. And his wife, Elsie, called Mickey a moral idiot.

But Elsie measures actions in terms of their practical consequences and offers her husband no more support. Years earlier, when he returned from the Soviet Union, Lou wrote a book on communism that, for Elsie's sake, he burned. The revised manuscript was published, but now, about to publish a textbook, Lou confesses that the first left out much of what he saw in Russia. In order to be true to Elsie and to the party, he lied. Now he wants to be true to himself, but Elsie is still a coward. When Mickey names Lou before the committee, Lou loses the support of his friends, but Quentin—prompted, he thinks, by love—defends him. Were Quentin's love uncompromised, he would not have cared, but when the news of Lou's suicide reaches him, he feels relief, even joy. More importantly, he admits his betrayal: when Lou acknowledges Quentin as his only friend, both he and Quentin understood that Lou saw through his faithfulness.

Throughout the final years of their marriage, Louise pleaded with Quentin to acknowledge her as a separate person. Suspicious over Quentin's relationships with women, defensive about her relationship with Quentin, irritated each time Quentin interrupts her at a party, Louise is undaunted in her refusal to doubt herself and insistent upon her separateness. But Louise's search for selfhood, assisted by psychoanalysis, is incomprehensible to Quentin, who cannot endure being a separate person. In surveying his past, Quentin identifies the moments at which his mother, Mickey, Lou, and Louise became separate people. But, like Lou, who committed suicide when he understood he was alone, Quentin laments that the "unseen web of connection between people is simply not there. And I always relied on it." By the end of act 1, Quentin tentatively admits, "I think I still believe it. That underneath we're all profoundly friends!"

Quentin sees life in terms of a balance sheet of debits and credits, of promissory notes and IOUs. Whether he is speaking of Felice's offer of love, of Lou's and Elsie's reactions when they learn that Mickey will name Lou before the Committee, of his mother's death, or of his sexual and marital relations with Holga or Louise, Quentin needs to keep his own accounts in balance. Louise, though, refuses to allow him innocence and will not accept guilt. In a moment of self-exposure, Quentin pleads with her: "If you would come to me and say that something, something important was your fault and that you were sorry . . . it would help."

Quentin is moving toward the recognition of communal complicity, of a guilt that everyone shares and that equalizes all accounts. Obsessed by a pressing sense of guilt for the wrecked lives in which he has participated, Quentin must come to understand that guilt is an essential of human nature — not an impediment to healthy relationships, but an honest acknowledgment of the Fall, to which all are legitimate heirs. With Holga, he walks through the memorial concentration camps, sensing complicity. Finally, he will see the camp as the contemporary equivalent of the experience of Eve and understand what Holga means when she says, "But no one is innocent they did not kill!"

Still, Quentin must work through the Maggie story, and by act 2 he is ready to do so. At the end of act 1, Maggie, sitting up in bed on an upper stage, calls to him. When the Listener returns from his break, Quentin begins her story.

Like Miller's own second wife, Marilyn Monroe,[9] Maggie is a voluptuous sex kitten, an entertainer of modest talent who attracts men on the street like a magnet and is sexually charitable with the multitudes. When she first met Quentin, she was working as a switchboard operator in the building that housed his law firm, and she was refreshed by the man's protectiveness and innocence: unlike other men she had encountered, Quentin did not proposition her.

Despite her sexual experience, Quentin sees Maggie as a woman of undaunted innocence. When she reappears in act 2, she is dressed in bridal white, promising to be good to Quentin but protesting that he need not make her his wife; she could simply come to him whenever he wanted her. Four years after their initial encounter, Maggie is an established singer, a sensuous voice who will soon be a millionaire. One fan, she tells Quentin, keeps her records in the refrigerator, afraid that her seething tones will melt them. Maggie's love for Quentin is at once childlike and selfless. She idolizes him, defines herself as Quentin's friend, and, unlike others with the balance-sheet mentality, expects nothing from him. Inviting Quentin to sleep with her, she asks:

> Can't somebody just give you something? Like when you're thirsty? And
> you drink, and walk away, that's all.
> QUENTIN: But what about you?
> MAGGIE: Well . . . I would have what I gave. (*CP2*, p. 204)

Maggie exhibits a similar generosity when she names her exploitative friends as her beneficiaries and when she signs autographs for young boys who taunt her. Her first direct verbal expression of love is an inflamed "I love you, Quentin. I would do anything for you. And I would never bother you, I swear."

But Maggie's innocence proves more a psychological aberration than a primeval condition, and perhaps Quentin recognizes this all along. To the Listener, he confesses, "Fraud—from the first five minutes! . . . Why did I lie to her, play this cheap benefactor." More and more frequently, Maggie sees smoke coming out of the closet, explaining to Quentin that her mother, who was "very moral," got dressed in the closet, sometimes smoking in it, and, when she emerged, there would be a cloud of smoke around her. Maggie tells Quentin about her attempt to contact her father, who had left when she was eighteen months old. She took a train upstate, where he ran a business, and called him from the station, only to have the man deny paternity and tell her to see his lawyer. Maggie only wanted him to see her, and, when he refused, she walked around the town, fantasizing about being picked up by him, "Cause my mother said he always liked beautiful girls!":

QUENTIN: And then you'd tell him?
MAGGIE: I don't know. Maybe. Maybe . . . afterwards. (*CP2*, p. 197)

Maggie's premoral behavior and limited intelligence are so apparent that strangers and friends find it easy to take advantage of her. Maggie's agents, Jerry and Andy, contrive a will that leaves Maggie's money to the agency, yet they refuse to get her the piano player she prefers until Quentin intervenes. Maggie defends her vulnerability as trust, but Quentin increasingly recognizes her need to be victim. From the beginning, Quentin sees himself as moral and psychological guide. But under Quentin's tutelage, Maggie learns to speak and to understand: "I'm a joke that brings in money." She is even able to turn Quentin's own counsel on him: "You're like a little boy, you don't see the knives people hide."

Maggie has moved through innocence into experience, to a clearer yet more muddled concept of self that she does not like and cannot accommodate. Nostalgic for the time when Quentin protected and defended her, when love was pure and unencumbered, Maggie turns to alcohol, sleeping pills, and suicide attempts, each a plea to Quentin to take responsibility for her life.

But Quentin refuses to be her victim or to allow her to be his. After fifteen or so sleeping pills, Maggie hands the bottle to Quentin, but he will not take it. He will not receive her as his victim. With Maggie's suicide just over a year old, Quentin must articulate his relationship to her death before he can accept Holga. He remembers telling Maggie that they used one another and "loved each other's innocence as though to love enough what was not there would cover up what was." The paradox is that in his attraction to her prelapsarian innocence, Quentin has imposed upon himself a postlapsarian responsibility for her life. As Maggie attempts suicide for the third time, he must abjure both her innocence and his guilt. He is not guilty for her life, but he is responsible for his own. Within the context of inherent guilt and communal responsibility, Quentin acknowledges, "We are all separate people," bound by choice. Quentin's final vision accommodates guilt as a given of human nature, responsibility as a necessity of human experience, and love as the guarantor of hope.

Quentin is ready to respond to Holga's hello. Walking through the mental landscape of his life, past Louise, his family, his friends, and Maggie, he holds out his hand to Holga, who had long ago learned "one must finally take one's life in one's arms." As Albert Wertheim perceptively observes,

For Holga acceptance replaces judgment: acceptance of the deformity and idiocy in life: acceptance of the fact that the environs of Salzburg can house the disgrace of a concentration camp and the achievement of Mozart; and that one can go from the complex feelings engendered by a visit to the edifice of evil, the concentration camp, to the simplistic triumph of pure good.[10]

As a separate person with the responsibility of choice, as a participant in the moral relatedness of humankind, and as an occupant of a postlapsarian world, Quentin, hopeful, returns Holga's hello.

8

❖❖

Incident at Vichy

Throughout the self-indulgent therapeutic session in *After the Fall*, Miller neutralizes Quentin's paralyzing sense of guilt, allowing him to reject individual obsession, accept complicity, and once again embrace personal choice. Still intrigued by the question of culpability, Miller moves in *Incident at Vichy* from the private landscape of Quentin's mind to the historical forum of Vichy, France, with the same conclusion. But here the emphasis is less on the understanding of individual guilt as inescapably but acceptably human than on the universal attribution of a moral culpability usually reserved for a few. The play is brutally insistent upon a guilt that refuses to discriminate, a guilt suggested by Holga's acknowledgment that, since the concentration camp, no one can be innocent. It is a guilt affirmed by Miller's sobering report on the Frankfurt Nazi trials of 1964, written for the *New York Herald-Tribune*:

The question in the Frankfurt courtroom spreads out beyond the defendants and spirals around the world and into the heart of every man. It is his own complicity with murder, even the murders he did not perform himself with his own hands. The murders, however, from which he profited if only by having survived.[1]

The German concentration camp tower that intrudes upon Quentin's personal memories in *After the Fall* becomes a suggestive presence in *Incident at Vichy* as the postlapsarian corruption of humankind locates itself more insistently in the Nazi experience.

Based on a story Miller had heard some years earlier, *Incident at Vichy* dramatizes a daily occurrence in 1942 France: the systematic rounding up of suspected Jews and other undesirables by the Vichy government as it yielded to German racial laws. On this particular morning, eight men and a boy have been corralled into a detention center and lined up on a bench, none of them sure why. The play records the suspicions, the misgivings, the self-assurances, and the delusions of the Jews who know their identity papers are false but refuse to believe in the death camp.

Like Beckett's archetypal pair in *Waiting for Godot*, Miller's characters wait in the detention space, talking a bit in the process, and, more importantly, creating as a defense the illusion of their significance. The abducted of Miller's play are trapped in a situation from which there is no exit, yet they continue to pretend that freedom will come. As the prisoners wait to be summoned individually into the adjacent room, where the identity check takes place, they deny the desperation of circumstance, replacing despair with hope even as it becomes increasingly clear that there is none.

But the vision of Miller's play extends to a judgment of human nature not as helpless occupant of an arbitrary world in which there is nothing to be done but as heir to a moral depravity that demands action and accountability from everyone. No one in Miller's sorry group of oppressors and oppressed escapes blame: all are participants in a human shame incapable of being collectively or individually denied. If the judge's bench is empty in *After the Fall*, here the seat is occupied by Arthur Miller, presiding as moral judge over all humankind.

The obvious oppressors in *Incident at Vichy* are the single armed guard who prevents the abducted from walking down the corridor and out the door; the Major, who, having been injured in combat, now follows orders and interrogates; the detectives, who round up suspects on the streets; and the Professor, who has devised the simplest, most effective means of determining Jewishness: through exposing the circumcised penis. But Ferrand, who brings the Major coffee and whispers to the Waiter of the death furnaces, is an oppressor as well. Symbolic of the hundreds of thousands of French people who outnumber the Germans but endorse, through their silence, the Germans' barbarity, Ferrand will not risk his own life to save others; defending his inaction to the Waiter, he asks his friend, "What can I do?" reminding him, "I told you fifty times to get out of this city!"[2] Lebeau, hungry, anxious, and unkempt, also qualifies; wishing he were Von Berg, whose uncircumcised penis will be his freedom pass, the artist allows himself to feel guilty for being a Jew. Bayard, the electrician who has seen the death trains, prepares himself for deportation, breaking off the Gypsy's pot handle to pry open the train door from the inside. Monceau, the actor, deludes himself into believing he will live in peace if he obeys the law; for him, it is important not to look like a victim.

Even the Old Jew, the most obvious candidate for extermination, is an accomplice. Mad or heroic—"to walk around with a beard like that in a country like this!"—the Old Jew silently screams for the dignity of Jews, insisting upon a tribal identity that can only mean the death camp. Yet in his silence he becomes as much oppressor as oppressed: the bundle he clings to is filled with feathers, which float vacantly around the space. Immobile, he sits in silence as the Major reproaches both the Old Jew and himself. In Miller's terms, the Old Jew's willingness to be victim, reflected in his and the other characters' refusal to act, converts innocent victims to guilty conspirators, extending culpability to all.

Leduc, the one character who understands this, attempts to rally the group's strength and jump the guard. But each has a different reason for not joining him: Lebeau has not eaten since the previous day, the Boy is not strong enough, Von Berg's hands are of no use, Monceau will not risk his life for nothing—this despite Bayard's report that he has seen trains with Polish engineers and people locked inside. Even when Ferrand whispers to the prisoners that their destiny is a concentration camp, no one will act. As long as your papers are in order you are safe. . . . They let Marchand the businessman go, didn't they? . . . The Gypsy probably stole the pot. . . . It's not in the best interest of the Germans to kill Jews; they need labor. . . . How can a people who love music be capable of such atrocity? . . . If they were engaged in so systematic a round-up of Jews, why would they have only one guard at the door? . . . "That is the most fantastic idiocy I ever heard in my life!" Leduc recognizes that "they rely on our own logic to immobilize ourselves," which, clearly, it does. No one jumps the guard; each is condemned to death.

Aside from Marchand, the businessman who is given a white pass and apparently is not a Jew—though he may well be a Jew who is working with the government—each of the prisoners in turn is sent off until only Von Berg and Leduc remain. Though late additions to the club of the condemned, the pair become the play's central characters and, each in his own way, a hero of the occasion. Von Berg, apparently picked up because he had an unusual accent, is Catholic, a member of the Austrian nobility, a man whose cousin is deeply involved with the Nazis and who has until now dismissed Nazism as a vulgarity. When called by Leduc to bear witness to his rank and his family, he comes to admit that cultivated people become Nazis, that the furnaces do exist, and that nothing any longer is forbidden. Finally, though, he will not accept paralysis and becomes capable of the one heroic gesture of the morning: having cleared up the misunderstanding surrounding his arrest, he gives his white pass of freedom to Leduc.

Leduc, a former French combat officer and a psychiatrist, is a voice of protest and reason. Having studied the human mind professionally, five years formally in Germany and Austria, Leduc understands the capabilities of his oppressors and the psychology that assures their success. When he learns that the identity check is not of papers but of penises, a near-foolproof method to identify Jews anatomically, Leduc urges an assault on the armed guard, but fear and trust in the rational prevent the others from agreeing. Every one of the interred fears the unspeakable evil that he can neither accommodate into his vision of human nature nor admit will dictate his fate. Refused assistance by everybody but the Boy, Leduc confronts the German Major conducting the interrogation, the man who lost his leg at Amiens and now is only doing his job. Leduc will believe the Major's expression of incredulity only if the Major shoots himself and the oppressors. But the Major will not allow Leduc a greater claim to life than his own. Not having succeeded in his call for resistance either among the condemned or with the Major, Leduc reproaches himself for not acknowledging the darkness of human nature, for rationalizing evil and deluding himself into concealing the truth.

But in the play's final moments, Von Berg sacrifices his freedom, and possibly his life, for Leduc. Even as the Prince's gesture redeems the play's vision of humankind, however, Leduc's acceptance of the gesture neutralizes it. When the psychiatrist challenges the Major's commitment to his task, claiming himself a better man because he could not do what the Major is doing, the Major asks whether he would refuse the coveted white pass that would admit him to freedom; Leduc cannot in honesty say that he would. The Major pushes Leduc further, discrediting his claim of moral superiority by acknowledging that Leduc would not only leave, he would do so with relief and even delight—while the others remained behind. When Von Berg offers him the pass, Leduc hesitates for a moment, claiming he was not asking Von Berg for it.

But perhaps Leduc *was* asking for the pass all along. He is, after all, a psychiatrist, trained in understanding human behavior and surely capable of manipulating it. Since joining the captives, Leduc has been strenuously encouraging action on the part of his colleagues that could result in his escape. When Monceau tells of how he tried to dispose of forbidden books but was caught because he had forgotten that his name was stamped in each of them, Leduc suggests that Monceau knew all along about the names and simply wanted to get caught. When he asks Von Berg to tell his wife he will not return, he wants her to know about the furnaces, later withdrawing his request when he admits it was intended to injure a woman he no longer loved.

Leduc's willingness to take the risk of an attempted escape may well be motivated by more than the French Jew's desire to support the cause of all Jews or by his attempt to restore pride in Jewishness and faith in France. It may, finally, be a merely selfish desire to save his own life, even at the expense of others. Leduc has no way of knowing whether those he is encouraging are also Jews, nor does he try to find out; he simply demands that they risk their lives. And, finally, when offered the pass that may well mean the death of Von Berg, Leduc proves the Major right; he leaves the detention center, his heart relieved.

A number of critics of this play have objected to Miller's inclusive condemnation, reasoning that, if all are guilty, then all are innocent. Philip Rahv's essay, "Arthur Miller and the Fallacy of Profundity," reflects this belief:

Responsibility cannot be other than specific: if all are responsible none are responsible. It is simply not true that we are all responsible for the Nazi horrors, and to universalize in this fashion the German guilt is to transfer it to human nature in general and thus vaporize it. The argument from human nature in general is insubstantial because it is so exceedingly vague, explaining everything and nothing at the same time.[3]

Whether or not Miller's judgments are plausible or earned, critics dismissed *Incident at Vichy* as a moral lecture. Julius Novick remarked that "Miller does not really want to write plays any more; he wants to talk to us directly." Henry Hewes called the piece "an illustrated essay," while Robert Brustein chided the playwright for giving us "not so much a play as another solemn sermon on Human Responsibility."[4] More recent critics, though less offended by the play's self-righteousness, are equally unwilling to acknowledge its special strength. Dennis Welland, for example, complains that the play is static, it has too many coincidences—the Major knows Leduc and the Waiter—and it hosts too large a cast.[5]

But *Incident at Vichy* deserves a second look: exquisitely crafted, the play moves like a sonata, restrained, occasionally erupting into energy, sounding its melody and repeating it in variation. Its first segment, the animated monologue of Lebeau, prodding the others into conversation, builds to the moment when the interrogators enter, adding Leduc, Von Berg, and the Old Jew to the group. The men wait through the adagio, as Marchand, the businessman who looks like a Jew, is questioned and released. The scherzo is the quick succession of interviews of the Gypsy, Bayard, the Waiter, Monceau, Lebeau, the Boy, and the Old Jew, each culminating in condemnation. And the last movement, again allegro, is the pointed dialogue between the remaining two men, Leduc and Von Berg, which climaxes in the Prince's giving his pass to the Jew.

Like *A Memory of Two Mondays*, *Incident at Vichy* is a quintessentially modern play, operating in an inner space of movement and mood. Like *After the Fall*, it gives voice once again to the concern with culpability that Miller first expressed dramatically some thirty years earlier in the University of Michigan plays. Here, as elsewhere, Miller's dramatic voice echoes Leduc's demand of Von Berg: "It's not your guilt I want, it's your responsibility—that might have helped." Defining the Jew as "other" and acknowledging that all people, even Jews, know themselves through knowing who they are not, Leduc implores Von Berg to "see that you have yours — the man whose death leaves you relieved that you are not him, despite your decency. And that is why there is nothing and will be nothing — until you face your own complicity with this . . . your own humanity." If this is the measure of guilt for Miller, then there are no innocents, but Miller's sympathy for the fallen is unashamed.

9

••

The Price

Martin Gottfried, reviewing a New York revival of *The Price*, called Miller's 1968 play "self-imitation." The revival "only aggravated [his] sense of loss and bewilderment," convincing him that Miller was deferring—even selling out—to public taste. *The Price*, Gottfried claimed, was "peculiar in using a style that Miller considered too old-fashioned long ago. So anxious was he to please."[1]

Gottfried acknowledges the nonrealistic style of a number of Miller's plays but, finally, yields to what would appear a critical conspiracy to dismiss Miller as a realistic playwright, as yet unweaned from Ibsen. In a number of ways, the play is indeed self-imitation, continuing the playwright's dialogue with the family and with the past. Connecting once again with Miller's own biography, the drama of two brothers, reunited for the sale of their dead parents' furniture, brings together the themes and the concerns of Miller's earlier work: guilt, moral debt, self-delusion, success, choice and consequence, and conflicting moral principle. Even unsigned, the play bears the unmistakable signature of Arthur Miller.

Yet *The Price* is quite unlike *All My Sons*, the one play Miller agrees is Ibsenesque. A vestige of the well-made play, *All My Sons* develops in well-crafted, interrelated segments, extending its exposition throughout much of the action and revealing information about the past a patch at a time until it reaches closure of action and moral resolution. *The Price*, on the other hand, develops in sustained, almost leisurely segments that work less at complicating action than at deepening character. Though there is much discussion of moral position, neither of the two brothers changes his commitment, and the drama ends with only the sales transaction resolved. Moreover, Miller's junk dealer, Gregory Solomon, teases

the audience into a symbolic reading of this octogenarian Jew with
whom the brothers must come to terms in their transaction with the
past.

The Price takes place in the attic of a Manhattan brownstone.
Ten rooms of furniture and assorted personal belongings of the
dead Franzes have been warehoused there for years. Because the
building is scheduled for demolition, Victor Franz and his wife,
Esther, have returned to this physical and emotional stockpile to
negotiate with Solomon for its sale. Though Walter Franz does not
join his brother until act 2, he is, by inference, already a character in
act 1, when dialogue reveals that the brothers' professional lives are
the consequence of opposite decisions they made years before.
When their father was driven into financial and psychological desti-
tution by the stock-market crash, the self-sacrificing Victor gave up
college and became a cop, while the self-interested Walter pursued a
medical career.

The two brothers participate in a moral fencing match that
scores no palpable hits and ends where it began. During the match
Walter reveals a piece of information that he is convinced will
change Victor's assessment of the past: though the family ate garbage, their father was not bankrupt after all, having squirreled away
several thousand dollars that he used to live on and to provide the
security he had been robbed of by the Depression. Had Victor
known about the money, he might not have had to spend twenty-
eight years on the police force nor reached a point in middle age
when his life's achievements seemed small. Earlier in his career,
Miller would have made this revelation a turning point, but here he
has Victor respond not with bitterness and disbelief but with an
understanding that will not permit him to invalidate his life.
Love and moral responsibility had motivated Victor earlier; now,
despite his new knowledge, he can only affirm the rightness of what
he did.

Walter, on the other hand, showed little compassion for his
father, knowing the older man deceived his sons into thinking he
could not help them through college. Seeing in his father a model of
self-interest, Walter pursued a medical career, sending home only a
nominal amount of money each month after he was established. But
in the process of becoming and being a surgeon, Walter has suffered

mental and marital collapse. Three years earlier, he was hospitalized with a mental breakdown; now divorced, he is clearly disappointed that his sons find guitars more intriguing than college. Despite the difference in the brothers' circumstances and positions, the play does not prefer either one morally. As Miller notes of the brothers, "If you extend their characteristics into the world, you see that neither one of them could run the world. The things that can be done by Walter, full of daring, selfishness, power, lust, and inventiveness, are not the things the other one can do, which is to stick to a job that needs to be done, stay by the hearth and see to it that the fire doesn't go out."[2] The brothers exist in an equilibrium, their commitments to opposing but complementary moral postures balanced by a common fear for their own psychic lives. Indeed, life seems to have passed both brothers by, Victor because he was never able to live it the way he would have liked, Walter because he lived it at too accelerated a pace, until he "eliminated anything extraneous . . . including people."[3]

When they meet for the first time in sixteen years, both are ready to dispose of their inheritance. Collectively, the harp, the bureaus, the buffet, the dining-room table, the phonograph, the lap robe, the opera hat are worth only $1,100 to Solomon. Victor, who has invested years in his father's life, could use the cash; his father's furniture should, his wife reasons, bring them some leisure. But Victor's sense of fair play tells him to divide the profits with his brother, even though the surgeon is financially secure. As always, Victor will not be accused of selfishness; his account book will always honor what others deserve. But Walter not only wants no part of the price of the furniture, he even offers an alternative arrangement whereby he will donate the collection to the Salvation Army, claim a tax deduction, and split the savings on his federal income tax with his brother. Victor considers the option but, finally, rejects it, honoring his deal with Solomon.

The transaction with Solomon, of course, has greater value than cash, providing the brothers with the occasion for defending their moral positions. Victor, in accepting a figure below the collection's value and in insisting that half belongs to Walter, continues the self-sacrificing behavior that prompted him to care for his father, while Walter, in refusing his share and extending the counteroffer, may well be trying to settle his moral debt and to buy his way back into the family.

Yet in a curious way, both brothers are trying to buy their way *out* of the family. Walter has felt all along that there was no love between father and sons, whereas Victor, perhaps to legitimize his commitment, has insisted there was. Now, in the presence of those objects that defined their earlier lives, the two attempt to dispose not only of the artifacts of their heritage but of their father as well. As Miller comments,

> The brothers are trying to exorcise the multiple meanings of things made on their lives, to clear them, negate them. Of course it's not possible—that's also the price. They are their father's sons, he's in them. . . . They'll never rid themselves of their father.[4]

If Walter fails to settle the debts of the past by offering his brother first the income tax deal and then a position in hospital administration, he nonetheless seems satisfied. In the Depression years, when Victor was living with his father, the younger man appealed to Walter for a five-hundred-dollar loan that would enable him to get through college. But Walter, knowing their father could provide it, refused. The consequence for Victor was an aborted education and over twenty years of living with and supporting the father. Clearly Walter feels a nagging sense of responsibility for Victor's life, yet his tendering of the two latest offers seems enough to assuage him, even though Victor will not accept. Walter tells his brother, he has offered him everything he knows how to.

In recovering from his mental breakdown, Walter apparently developed emotional defenses that he has become skilled at applying. In the showdown with his brother, he repeats what a therapist undoubtedly helped him to believe: that Victor made his own choices, that he did not steal his brother's life. Walter may have convinced himself that Victor, not he, is responsible for his brother's choice, but he clearly cannot understand his brother's motivation. When Victor refuses the hospital job, saying he cannot trust his brother, Walter assesses the rejection as vengeance. Nor can he accommodate the possibility of moral principle explaining why Victor devoted nearly all of his life to their father. Seeing the father as

manipulative and exploitative, he decides, "He was smarter than all of us—he saw what you wanted and he gave it to you!" . . . [to Solomon] "Go ahead, you old mutt—rob them blind, they love it!"
Walter is good at labeling human action, poor at understanding the complexity of human nature. Victor, on the other hand, comes face to face with what his brother has known all along: that his family life may not have been worth protecting. But in their confrontation, Victor comes to know that, whether or not he is a masochist and whether or not he spent his life trying to defend his father's love, he did something essentially human and good.

When the brothers part, Walter is wrapped in his expensive camel-haired coat, Victor is wearing his gun belt and cop's jacket. Their uniforms are as different and as irreconcilable as their moral positions, each serving as visual symbol of personal choice.

It is clear that for each of the brothers, the final settlement is neither with Solomon nor with the other brother but with himself, a circumstance that Victor's wife, Esther, must also come to understand. Until Victor's confrontation with Walter, Esther had been pressuring him to retire, to spend some vacation time with her, to start a new career more lucrative than the first. A practical but self-pitying woman on the edge of alcoholism, Esther saw little virtue in her husband's commitment to his father and much virtue in his bargaining with the junk dealer for the best price on the furniture. When Walter reveals the fact that the father had four thousand dollars, she is outraged. But as she listens to the argument between the physician and the cop and to Walter's assessment of Victor, she finds herself defending their life. Earlier ashamed of her husband's uniform, she now asks him not to change into his business suit for their night at the movies, endorsing, as Victor has, a life that was not, after all, a waste.

Victor's and Esther's discovery does not end with their reconciliation with their past lives; it continues into a vision of a new life, perhaps the product of Victor's retirement or, more likely, of their perspective on his present commitment. For a long time, Victor has felt that he was deluding himself by thinking that at age fifty he could begin anything. But Solomon, the dealer, is eighty-nine, and in buying the furniture he is making a commitment that will not only put him back in the furniture business but will also require a substantial investment of time. Nor will this be Solomon's first new beginning: he was married at nineteen, twenty-two, fifty-one, and seventy-five; he lost all his money in 1898, 1904, 1923, and 1932; he lived in six countries and nearly got killed more than once. Solomon brings to Victor a model of resiliency and an optimism Victor has not felt since he began college. The old man had his share of sadness—he twice recalls the suicide of his young daughter, for which he feels a lingering responsibility: "Maybe I could have said something to her . . . maybe I *did* say something." But as he remarks later, "But if it was a miracle and she came to life, what would I say to her?"

Wise, lovable, and shrewd, Solomon expresses what he knows about life in the idiom of his profession: the modern mentality equates disposable with beautiful, shopping with salvation. The Franz furniture, he contends, is too sturdy to be sellable: "If it wouldn't break there is no more possibilities. . . . A man sits down to such a table he knows not only he's married, he's got to stay married—there is no more possibilities."

"Possibilities" has been what Solomon's life has been about: his profession is one of speculation and trust. Every transaction, whether in business or in life, is a bargain, and Solomon, despite frequent loss and constant risk, has entered into each new contract with faith. Whether on stage or off, resting in the bedroom while the brothers talk, Solomon is a presiding presence in the play.

The man, in fact, is one of Miller's most beautifully articulated characters. A prize for any character actor, the role draws upon stereotypical Jewishness and avuncularity, adding personality touches that have little to do with plot but leisurely round out the masterful portrait. There is no urgency in Solomon's professional style; though he is quick to assess the value of the furniture, he tactfully delays the offer, pausing to question Victor, to speak of his own personal life, and to eat snacks he carries in his briefcase.

But even as Solomon functions as an irresistibly delightful character, Miller insists on his symbolic dimension as well. Refer- ring to a review of a production at the Spoleto USA Festival, Miller notes that the critic "likened Solomon to the Dybbuk of Jewish folklore, a spirit who inhabits human bodies until he is exorcised."[5] As purchaser of the family possessions, Solomon takes title to the

Franz brothers' past, remaining in the attic with the furniture as Walter and Victor leave.

Interestingly, though the furniture has remained untouched since their father's death, neither is willing to abandon it to the demolition crew. And while neither wants to select pieces of furniture to keep—pieces of the past to incorporate into the present—their affection for the furniture is manifest. Defensive about its financial worth, they are, in fact, insisting on a value to which Solomon can affix no price. Finally, in disposing of the furniture to the dealer, Victor, at least, feels as though he is placing it in trust, with a trustee who will keep some pieces and selectively distribute the rest. Without destroying the past, he has succeeded in removing its heavy burden. In coming to terms with Solomon, Victor has come to terms with himself.

Miller refers to *The Price* as "a quartet":

The integrity of the parts is very exact, very intense. If one of them is off it just doesn't work. It's probably the most specific play I've ever written, the most intensely carved.[6]

Although he divides the play into two acts, he prefers that a production be continuous. When it is not, the first act ends with the two brothers, meeting after sixteen years, shaking hands, the second with the end of that handshake.

Both acts are divided into two parts. The first part of act 1, in which Victor and Esther wait in the attic for the dealer to arrive, is expository: it reveals Victor's relationship to his brother, to his dead father, and to his wife. Esther is especially insistent in this early scene on measuring life in monetary terms. For three years, she has been prodding her husband into retiring from the police force. Had he begun graduate school three years ago, he would be ready now to enter a higher-paying profession. Esther does not want Victor to wear his uniform to the movies, for she sees it as a banner announcing their poverty. She is frank in her admission that she wants more money than they have, encouraging her husband to see his brother as a debtor and to cultivate a relationship with this "rich and influential" man. Though clearly bitter about their circumstances, Es-

ther still feels great affection for her husband and wants him to start
again as much for his sake as for hers. But Victor is less ready to
take risks, and their presence now among the material clutter in
which they lived after his father lost his fortune reminds him of the
caution that has characterized his life. Surveying the remnants of his
father's life, Victor recalls how the once-wealthy businessman was
reduced to eating garbage after the crash just as he, once an aspiring
and talented science student, wound up in civil service. Being
among the unused objects of opulence is painful for both Esther
and Victor, who are at once conscious of the division between the
rich and the poor and of how this room of furniture, which the
father might just as well have sold years ago, has shaped their lives.
The segment ends, though, in a moment of affirmation of their
relationship. Victor, in fencing gear, assumes the posture of the
fencer as Esther cries her admiration.

Solomon, catching his breath and coughing after the long
climb, interrupts them, and the unorthodox bargaining session begins. As Esther leaves the two men alone, Victor asks Solomon,
"Will you be very long?" and Solomon replies, "With furniture you
never know, can be short, can be long, can be medium." In fact,
Solomon's eye is quick, his judgment sure; it is not his assessment of
the furniture but his assessment of the seller that will determine how
long the transaction will be, for Solomon wants to be very sure
when he makes the offer that it will hold. The dealer's strategy is
transparent but splendid: in between shrewd gazes at the furniture,
he flatters Victor's wife, tells stories of his life, testifies to his long
years in the business, makes jokes, eats an egg, and seduces Victor
into talking about his father and about himself. It is important to
Solomon that he establish his trustworthiness on a personal level so
Victor will believe him when he devalues the furniture. Though
undeniably handsome, most of the furniture simply has no contemporary appeal: people do not want such bulky furniture any more; it
does not pass through the new apartment doors. And the sound-
board on the harp is cracked.

But Solomon is doing more than writing the terms of the bargain; he himself is following through on a decision that will affect
his life. Victor must have used an old phone book when he looked
up the dealer's number, for Solomon, expecting he would soon die,

retired years before. But unlike Victor's father, who never could "bounce back," Solomon is resilient enough to restart life at eighty-nine. Having evoked Victor's sympathy and his admiration, Solomon makes an offer below the prevailing market price, which Victor, after some resistance, accepts. When Solomon explains to Victor that "the price of used furniture is nothing but a viewpoint, and if you wouldn't understand the viewpoint is impossible to understand the price," he is counseling Victor on a philosophy of life even as he employs it. The segment ends with Solomon handing hundred-dollar bills to Victor; he is about to place the eighth in his palm when Walter arrives.

The handshake that begins act 2 is a handshake of greeting, not agreement. It is the prelude to two segments, the first on renegotiation of the price, the second, more critical, on the brothers' attempt to come to terms with each other. The renegotiation begins with Walter's entrance and his distrust of Solomon. Though it is clear that he thinks $1,100 is too little for the furniture, he refrains from active disagreement until Esther appears. Then, hearing her disapproval, he joins with her in an attempt to get Solomon to raise the price. Walter had three-thousand dollars in mind, Esther $3,500. When the two fail to get Solomon to modify his offer, Walter proposes the income tax deal which will bring Victor as much as twelve-thousand dollars. Both renegotiations are still pending when Walter moves the act into its last segment with the query, "We don't understand each other, do we?"

The negotiation in the last segment of the play is not financial but moral, and it is Walter who needs to make a deal. Speaking of the terror he felt of experiencing the same financial disaster as their father, Walter explains how his breakdown led him to a new way of life, a slower, more-savored life that included friendship. But his job offer suggests that Walter is living by the same moral values as before: he is not providing Victor with a position for Victor's sake but for his own. Esther thinks that Walter is asking for Victor's friendship, but Victor sees the gesture differently. The physician is using his wealth to heal the injury for which he is unable consciously to accept any blame.

When Victor resists the offer, Walter becomes ruthless in his truth telling, revealing not only that he offered, through their father, to lend Victor five hundred dollars but that their father had money of his own. He is most ruthless when he bullies Victor into admitting that he suspected, even knew, all along that the father had money. Even as Victor is forced into being honest with himself, he recognizes Walter's relentless self-justification. And he will not yield to it.

Walter has come to see himself and Victor as two halves of the same person, and he wants Victor to validate his own vision of self. Both of them, he contends, were in the same trap and, in self-defense, invented selves. But what Victor pretended to be upholding he was actually denying. Walter needs that admission of denial to be whole. But Victor will not agree to the bargain: "You came for the old handshake, didn't you! The okay! . . . Well, you won't get it, not till I get mine!" The moral negotiation ends without agreement, for the brothers have nothing to give one another. There remains only the financial bargain between Victor and Solomon, which the two conclude.

Victor and Esther leave Solomon alone in the attic, and he does just what Victor did to open the play. Turning to the phonograph, he plays an old Gallagher and Shean record, a sustained recorded laugh that challenges its listener to resist. Just as Victor had surrendered at the beginning of the play, so Solomon surrenders now, allowing his laughter to mingle with the record and resonate throughout the attic space. The junk dealer's laughter may well be an expression of triumph, a self-satisfied approval of a bargain well made, and it may carry with it a sardonic condemnation of the two brothers who were unable to settle their impossible bargain. Or the laugh may be the laughter of abandon, a prelude to the new life that the purchase of the furniture provides. Or it may be an absurd laugh at all humankind, insisting on the continuation of life when, like the stockpile of furniture, it all adds up to so little. Whatever its meaning, it is clear that Solomon, like the two brothers, knows the price that life demands.

10

The Creation of the World
and Other Business

In his study of modern American drama, C. W. E. Bigsby reports that an early draft of *The Price* is on file in the Miller collection at the University of Texas,[1] suggesting that Miller had thought seriously about the play some twenty years before he completed it. Published in 1968, the play's connection with Miller's earlier work speaks to the durability and the dramatic repeatability of his lifelong concerns. If even a first look at *The Price* urges identification with Miller, however, a similar look at his next play, *The Creation of the World and Other Business* (1972), yields quite different results: religious parody, in the form of an irreverent reworking of Genesis, would seem not to fit the profile.

Miller's only attempt at comedy invited critics to offer some comic comments of their own. Frank Rich, reviewing the 1983 musical revival of the play, *Up from Paradise*, began with his own parody:

In the beginning—or, to be precise, in 1972—Arthur Miller created *The Creation of the World and Other Business*, and Broadway saw that it was not good. But the admirably buoyant Mr. Miller did not rest.[2]

Assessing Stanley Silverman's music, which includes "merry use of barbershop, Baroque and gospel harmonies," Rich decided that "the score often sounds like liturgical fragments that God had the good sense to eliminate from His sanctified repertory."[3] John Simon, reviewing the original dramatic production, began his *New York* evaluation with this line: "It is not surprising that, having been praised to the skies for even his recent, sorry work, Arthur Miller

119

should assault the heavens with his new play, *The Creation of the World and Other Business*."[4]

Modeled on those sections of Genesis that relate the creation of Eve, the expulsion from paradise, and Cain's murder of Abel, *The Creation of the World* is in fact not other business for Miller but old business. In the story of Adam and Eve's loss of innocence, the playwright locates the source for the obsessive guilt that has permeated his work since the Michigan plays and found its deepest expression in *After the Fall*. And in the archetypal family, he discovers the Ur-version of brotherly love and envy, devoting the last of three acts to the quarrel between Cain and Abel and its unhappy resolution. Though unusually distinctive in mode, *The Creation of the World* is an integral piece of the Miller canon, a play that stands as thematic précis of all his work. As Miller himself commented, "There are reverberations of all my plays in this one. It's wry, but with an underlying earnestness."[5]

The cast of characters in *The Creation of the World* includes Adam and Eve, Cain and Abel, God, Lucifer, and three incidental Angels. The play begins in paradise after the creation of much of God's wonder, including Adam. The day, of course, is a perfect one, as they all are, and Adam, under God's supervision, is busy naming. This seems to be an *1* day: he names the lion, the lamb, and, though he later reconsiders, the labbit. But as he surveys the animal kingdom, he notices that he is unique among living creatures in his singularity: only he does not have a mate. Anticipating Adam's query as to why this is so, God confides that he has been considering making a woman and proceeds to put Adam to sleep so he may remove one of his ribs and do so. Neither God nor Adam is certain that he wants a woman in paradise, so they agree that the creation of Eve will be an experiment.

It is an experiment, of course, that proves fatal, for the young woman has an inquiring, skeptical mind and an insatiable curiosity. Hearing the rules of paradise—"Those are apples on that tree; you will not eat them"—she speaks her first word: "Why?"[6] The self-satisfied Adam shares with her the names he has attributed to fruits and animals, only to learn that Eve does not think his pomegranate looks like a pomegranate or his prndn like a prndn. Yielding on the prndn, he renames the creature "louse," pleased that Eve too is naming with 1's. But Adam's first concession leads to a more serious one: before the act is over, Eve will be pushing the apple into Adam's mouth, having tasted of the fruit herself and discovered her sensuality.

Clearly Eve is the dominant party in this relationship, though Adam is nominally so. And clearly too Eve has been singled out by God to be cursed. She and Adam are both cast out of paradise into a world in which they can no longer hear the grass growing, the shadows on the leaves, or the fish in the river, but Adam suffers only from separation from God. Eve must endure physical deformity, in the form of a swollen belly, and, eventually, the pain of childbirth. Outside of paradise, Adam dreams of how things were while Eve busies herself in intellectual musings on her swelling. Adam is content with the explanation that she ate too many clams, but Eve suspects there is more to the thing within than that. And Lucifer, of course, responds to Eve's receptivity.

In fact, Lucifer has responded to Eve before—about nine months before—when at twilight he came to her. The thing within is not the son of Adam but of Lucifer, whose copulation with Eve has fulfilled God's command to her to multiply. When Lucifer attempts to enter the pregnant Eve again, however, she rejects him, turning to the sleeping Adam. But by now Lucifer has had his victory.

Eve's communion with Evil is the product not only of her curiosity and her sensuality but of Adam's neglect. Repulsed by her swollen form, Adam has had no desire for sex since they were expelled from paradise. And in paradise, he was unable to discriminate between what was good and what was very good. As Lucifer points out to God, Adam would just as soon pick his nose as make love to Eve. Adam takes such pleasure in kissing trees that he is unable to figure out what to do with the penis that he, but not Eve, possesses.

Miller's play is particularly harsh on Eve as progenitor of evil, yet it establishes her as an independent, intellectual female, celebrating both her mind and her body, taking command over matters of importance, and, finally, being cursed for her boldness. Hardly the passive female, Eve is the archetypal decision maker, whose choices determine the future of the world.

So also is Eve the "mother of mankind" and God's "favorite girl." When Chemuel, the Angel of Mercy, delivers her, God sees the newborn, sixteen-year-old Cain as innocence restored. Act 2 ends with an angelic waltz in which God sweeps Eve across the stage. But the innocence God thinks he has restored through Cain is only an illusion, for God does not yet know that Lucifer fathered the child, nor does he see Lucifer kiss the inert Cain to begin his life. In fact, God has cause to be distressed, as he is in act 3. The fact that people hardly mention his name anymore is the least of his troubles. Before Cain kills his brother, Eve will dance with Lucifer, accepting him as her God, and Cain and Eve will have sex.

The quarrel between Cain and Abel begins with the practical: Abel's sheep are eating Cain's corn; Cain wants Abel to fence in the sheep; Abel thinks Cain should fence in the corn. Upon counsel from Lucifer, however, Abel yields to his brother, hearing that he may avoid violence by doing so. But brotherly jealousy, God's curse, and Lucifer prevail, rendering Abel powerless to prevent his own death.

Cain rightfully feels that Eve loves Abel more than him, but he idealistically believes that he can restore the world's innocence. Hearing for the first time the story of Adam and Eve's expulsion from paradise—"We . . . didn't exactly *decide* to go, y'see. We were ah . . . told to leave"—Cain realizes that, rather than thanking God, they should be begging forgiveness.

Cain builds an altar to God and assembles a plate of fruit and vegetables to offer Him, even as Abel slays one of his lambs for the first Sabbath. The older brother is pleased that God likes his onion, disturbed that He savors Abel's mutton, and shattered when God refuses even to try his corn. Fraternal jealousy secures God's curse as Cain butchers his brother, introducing Death into the world.

If the emotional familiarity of familial life in the play is intriguing, the relationship between God and Lucifer is even more so. For throughout the play, from paradise to Death, the God of Evil opposes the God of Good. Lucifer's first argument to God is that innocence should be thinned out. Seeing that everything in paradise is equally good, he advises God to create a hierarchy of good so that Adam can discriminate. He is not yet bold enough to suggest the introduction of Evil, but when God accepts his volunteer help, he has in effect accomplished just that.

As with all literary Lucifers, this devil is vibrant and attractive, a far more exciting figure than his counterpart in Good. Lucifer's language is witty where God's is pedestrian, and his vitality makes God's more staid personality a bore. God's might is continually compromised by Lucifer's manipulations and by their discussions of God's master plan. This God is not only uncertain of his plan but is a bit inept in execution, and he is often surprised, relying on Lucifer for his intelligence. When, for example, Adam and Eve do not discover sex in paradise, God is content to wait. He does not wish to reconstruct woman, providing her with numerous apertures which man may enter, but trusts that, eventually, if only by accident, Adam will find the right place. Lucifer, on the other hand, the eternal actor and director, urges Eve to eat the apple, hastening the couple's discovery of sex. It is Lucifer who informs God that Eve is pregnant, and only later does he reveal that he was personally responsible for the conception.

By the end of act 1, Lucifer is proposing joint rule, arguing the complementarity of Good and Evil and the value of acknowledging both. Shrewd and manipulative, he offers to sit on God's right hand, or His left, simply for publicity, assuring God that He, not Lucifer, will actually be in charge. This victory, though, goes to God; seeing through Lucifer's plea, he rejects Evil, casting him into hell.

Later, in act 3, Lucifer will offer a counterproposal: he will be God of what-they-are; God will be in charge of their improvement. But, by this time, God has faced up to the inevitable: he will not have the last dance with Eve. Distressed over Lucifer's orchestration of Cain's murder of his brother, God yields victory and the world to Lucifer. Disillusioned, God does not want to be God anymore.

Despite Lucifer's triumph, though, Miller's play does not condemn the world it creates but rather passes judgment on the position of humankind given such a world. *The Creation of the World* ends with a chorus of denials by the founding family, none of whom will accept guilt nor take responsibility. Miller's literary obsession resonates once again, though this time apparently sounding the subject's exhaustion. Over the corpse of Abel, God despairs: "You are all worthless! The mother blames God, the father blames no one, and the son knows no blame at all." Not only will no one in this family admit guilt, but Cain points the finger of blame at God,

condemning His "justice" as arbitrary. When Eve laments the death
of her favorite son, Lucifer speaks his pragmatic truth: "There is no
consolation, woman! Unless you want the lie of God, the false tears
of a killer repenting!" God counters with the only argument he has
left, that love will redeem. As Miller commented, the play "proves
there is no possible rational ground for any hope whatsoever. . . .
And that's wonderful. There's nothing to do but go on living as
happily as possible."[7]

11

The Archbishop's Ceiling

In the afterword to the Methuen edition of *The Archbishop's Ceiling*, Christopher Bigsby calls that play, along with Miller's two recent one-act plays, *Some Kind of Love Story* and *Elegy for a Lady*, "a major new phase in the career of America's leading playwright." He hastens to add, "But the break is not as radical as it may appear"; Miller's earlier plays were governed by social and political concerns, important in *The Archbishop's Ceiling*, but they were also a prelude to this recent play's "fascination with the problematic status of the real."[1] Still, nowhere in the canon does Miller play with the complexities of truth and fiction with more urgency or more finesse than in *The Archbishop's Ceiling*. A sophisticated foray into the epistemological nature of reality and of art, the play combines and extends the private illusions of a Joe Keller or a Willy Loman and the public myths that control lives in *The Crucible* and *Incident at Vichy*. Miller's measure of truth, which ultimately is incapable of discriminating between the fictive and the real, is the world-stage metaphor, created through the presumed presence of hidden microphones in the archbishop's ceiling.

Though set in a small eastern European country, the play speaks to post-Watergate America, which, Bigsby points out, added a historical footnote to the more famous bugging of Democratic headquarters: in 1983, when the Mayflower Hotel in Washington, DC, a regular meeting place for politicians, was being renovated, construction workers discovered twenty-eight hidden microphones in the ceiling. In Miller's play, the ceiling of the former archbishop's residence, now government-owned, may or may not be miked, but the possibility that it is fundamentally affects the behavior and the thinking of at least one of the writers who assemble there. Under the archbishop's ceiling, Adrian Wallach casts life and fiction in a power struggle that unsettles the writer's assumptions and becomes Miller's apology for art.

Adrian has returned to this communist-controlled country for a brief visit with Maya, a woman he had spent time with before and who, when Marcus is away, lives in his house, under the archbishop's ceiling. An established, wealthy American writer, Adrian was attending a conference in Paris when he had a "blinding vision of the inside of [Maya's] thigh" and made arrangements to fly east. His mission is one of repossession, not only of Maya's body but of Maya, who will be the central character in his novel, and of the feeling of the country. After spending two years writing such a novel, he set it aside, unsatisfied:

I started out with a bizarre, exotic quality. People sort of embalmed in a society of amber. But the longer it got, the less unique it became. I finally wondered if the idea of unfreedom can be sustained in the mind. (*AC*, p. 66)

Now, as he speaks with Maya under the archbishop's ceiling, at first only vaguely aware of the possibility of microphones, he attempts to move out of his American mentality and into that of this paranoid country, in which writers are more often scorned as criminals than celebrated as heroes. Maya and Adrian talk of themselves and of Marcus and Sigmund, who later join them to discuss the crisis created by the government's confiscation of Sigmund's manuscript—an event that occurred since the writer had dinner with Adrian the evening before. Each of the characters must cope individually with the constant surveillance of the government, but the American visitor is most disturbed by it and by his growing knowledge that he can never have full access to anything he can satisfactorily call truth.

It has been two years since Adrian was last in this country; since that time he has talked with Allison Wolfe, who provided him with two pieces of factual or invented information: first, Maya and Marcus imported girls and held orgies for writers, whom they subsequently blackmailed; and, secondly, the ceiling in Marcus's house is bugged. Though Adrian knows his source is a gossip, the play begins with the somewhat tentative American alone in the archbishop's room, lifting the cushions and the lamp, peering into the open piano, and looking searchingly at the cherubim in the ceiling. The microphones become the arbiter of Adrian's behavior as he and the theater audience test the probability that the room is bugged and wonder about Maya and Marcus's relationship to the Secret Police that have possessed their private lives. Adrian speaks of an op-ed piece he wrote for the *New York Times* attacking this country, but Maya hardly reacts; when he pursues the issue further, she changes the subject: is she underwhelmed by an American writer's liberalism, expressed freely from outside her country's boundaries, or does she wish to protect her friend, who has also been her lover, from the listening ears?

If the possible presence of the microphone gives Adrian the feeling that he is counterfeiting his speech and if Maya's possible complicity creates an uncertainty in his trust, so also does a recent crisis in Adrian's personal life contribute to his doubts about human behavior and about art. Ruth, the woman he traveled with last trip and whom everyone always assumed was his wife, returned from this country severely depressed. But a pill reclaimed her, turning her into an active and productive woman, freed from the suicidal urge. Adrian connects the medication with the power of the government, questioning the control any human being ultimately has over his or her own life. And, just as seriously, he questions the validity of art that assumes psychology has something to do with human behavior.

Adrian's return to this country, then, is not simply a response to nostalgia or to lust, nor is it wholly an attempt to re-create the feelings he would like to record. It is the life-or-death quest of the artist to connect with a justifying truth that accommodates both his writing and life. As long as Adrian cannot validate the connection between motivation and behavior nor accept a power that neutralizes the human will, he cannot dispute Maya's contention that it is not necessary to write novels anymore. But his experience in this country repeatedly frustrates what he would like to believe about human behavior and, in turn, his faith in the validating power of art. For under the archbishop's ceiling, he sees fragments of what may be the truth, but he is unable to see anything whole.

Adrian's quest brings him in contact not only with Maya and Marcus, who may be government agents, but also with Sigmund, a dissident writer who takes masochistic pleasure in tempting the government to censure him and who will not leave the country even when threatened with imprisonment. Adrian never learns whether he can trust Maya and Marcus, whether Sigmund is courageous or foolish, or whether, as an American, he is capable of understanding what motivates any of them—if indeed even they can understand. He had left the pompous Parisian symposium on the contemporary novel and come to this country, to meet with writers who had actual troubles. But at the end of his stay, he can only repeat his original epistemological question:

Whether it matters anymore, what anyone feels . . . about anything. Whether we're not just some sort of . . . filament that only lights up when it's plugged into whatever power there is. (*AC*, p. 73)

Coming to terms with that power, whatever it may be, is fundamental to Adrian's quest. Ruth had not had the energy to dress herself, but now she swims fifty laps a day. The pill "plugged her into some . . . some power. And she lit up." But she has not changed; only her reaction to power has. Hearing Adrian's response to Ruth's experience, Maya tells him he need not write novels anymore, but Adrian knows that a writer has to write. Here in this country of sharply defined power, he may learn something about the compatibility or incompatibility of power and will. But even before he begins, Maya questions the purity of artistic expression, observing that she never met a writer who did not seek praise, success, and power.

Adrian does not know what to believe in this Eastern European country, but here he can test connections between motive and behavior and measure the capacity of art to validate truth. The fictional center of Adrian's abandoned novel is Maya, whom Adrian made a secret agent, operating in a country in which freedom is an illusion. Maya will also be the fictional center of the rewrite he plans, though in this version she and Marcus may well be underground champions of the literary world. Adrian pleads with Maya to cooperate, to expose herself freely in the next few days so that he may possess her in art. But Adrian finds no certainty in his life model and realizes during their interview that the fictional version of Maya he has created may indeed endorse life: she may be a secret agent after all.

Adrian's conversation with Maya urges him to modify his vision of her as a political idealist. Hostess of a radio show not on politics but on cooking, Maya spends much time numbing her brain with alcohol. But even when she is sober, she lives under the illusion that things are improving. When she hears that two plainclothesmen sat at the restaurant table next to Sigmund and Adrian, she blames Sigmund for having taunted the government by dining with an American writer. But Maya's willingness to compromise may extend even further: when Adrian speaks of Sigmund's manuscript, she follows him down the corridor to plead with him to return and to say, within the room, beneath the archbishop's ceiling, that he sent a copy of the manuscript to Paris. Though Adrian dearly wants to believe in Maya's goodness, when she coaxes him back into the room, he can only admit, in a complicated expression of elation and despair, that she has made him believe in his book.

Adrian's conclusion, though, is premature, as he himself knows, for Maya is more than the simple secret agent his abandoned novel creates. The lover of all three men—Adrian, Sigmund, and Marcus—the real Maya claims she does not know for certain whether the room is bugged, but, secret agent or not, she is a woman of complex motivation. Though "sorry for Socialism . . . for Marx and Engels and Lenin," Maya dismisses rebellion as unbecoming the middle-aged. A vestige of the woman's idealism breaks into the blurred vision of alcohol, as she speaks of Sigmund as their country's redeemer. But Maya ends her speech with practical advice to her would-be hero: "Go, darling. Please. There is nothing left for you."

The failed idealist practices her English by reading *Vogue*. Attracted to the vacant expressions of its girls and its unapologetic posture on success, she accepts the magazine as a definitive life text, containing only that which is true. Her manifesto carries a particular irony, for there is some evidence that the story about the orgies— whether or not they are connected with blackmailing writers—is true. When Marcus returns from London, he brings with him a young Danish woman, Irina, who, because she cannot speak English, becomes the embodiment of the *Vogue* woman: as the others agonize over what to do about Sigmund's manuscript, Irina plays the out-of-tune piano and sings "Bei mir bist du schoen," trying to liven up the party. But a world without responsibility is the same kind of wishful thinking Maya expresses when she suggests that they join the other children on the playground. Ironically but understandably, the middle-aged Maya prefers simplicity: the uncomplicated vision of *Vogue* or the admission by Sigmund that Alexandra, daughter of the minister of the interior, has thick legs.

After years of living under the archbishop's ceiling, of collaborating with Marcus either as a secret agent or as a friend of writers, Maya understands how Adrian can caution Sigmund against their lies, and she understands how Sigmund can defend lying as freedom.

But Adrian does not live in a country where illusion is an imperative of daily life—or at least he does not think he does. When Adrian observes the restrictions imposed on Sigmund as a writer, Maya can only respond, "My God—don't you understand *anything?*" The truth is that Adrian's simplistic vision of life and of art has led him to question both and to discard his latest artistic effort in frustration. Sigmund's paradox—that lying is our only freedom—is an eloquent defense of fiction and a sober acknowledgment that literature and life are both lies. But if life is a lie and fiction reflects it, then fiction is truth and is worth defending. The archbishop's ceiling becomes a powerful world-stage metaphor, transforming all human action into performance and endorsing the false even as it precludes the possibility that anything but the false can exist.

But within the world prescribed by the microphoned canopy, each of the characters creates, interprets, and revisions the truth, lying or not lying in order to shape an accommodating and an effective reality. The visitors do not know for certain whether the room is bugged or not, and the two residents—Maya and Marcus—claim that they do not know for sure either. Yet Marcus operates confidently beneath the cherubed plaster, using his power, which rests either in knowledge or in naïveté, to orchestrate action.

Marcus is a mysterious man, whom Adrian thought he knew

well. But when it came to writing a novel about him, the American realized he knew very little. Adrian is surprised to discover that Marcus spent six years in prison, amused to learn that the United States, fearing he was a Red spy, refused him admittance, while his own country, thinking him an American agent, arrested him on his return. Adrian has always thought Marcus a friend of writers— Marcus is a writer himself—but as the details of the confiscation of Sigmund's manuscript are disclosed, he finds himself challenging Marcus's veracity. How did Marcus hear of the confiscation in London? Has he returned to help Sigmund or to help the government achieve its purpose, which appears to be to force Sigmund to leave? Why, after all, has Marcus been afforded the privilege of travel and of residence in the former archbishop's home? Marcus reports that a government agent threatened him in London, saying Sigmund would be brought to trial. It would be a trial that, from Marcus's point of view, would be detrimental to his country's writers. He claims that he has returned to prevent such an occurrence, to plead with Sigmund to abandon heroics and, in the interest of others, to leave.

But Adrian becomes suspicious when he learns that Marcus has telephoned Alexandra, daughter of the man who would be in charge of the archbishop's ceiling were the place bugged. Sigmund is convinced that he is to be arrested and asks Adrian for help in securing Marcus's pistol. Thinking the idea foolish, Adrian reports it to Marcus, who offers his assessment of the government program: "Obviously—to drive him out of the country. Failing that, to make it impossible for him to function." Adrian lies to Marcus, telling him he sent a copy of Sigmund's manuscript to Paris on the morning flight. But Marcus catches him in the lie; there is no flight that day to Paris; Marcus knows that Adrian distrusts him. Outside the archbishop's room, he tells Adrian that he has always warned writers about the microphones; now Adrian challenges him to repeat this comment within the room. Later in the play, when Alexandra allegedly calls to report that the government is returning Sigmund's manuscript, Adrian is only further confused. He does not know whether this is part of the plan to get Sigmund to leave, whether Marcus is director of that plan, or whether his comments were indeed overheard and made a difference. Adrian needs to know what the gesture means, but Maya explains "it is nothing. . . . They have the power to take it and the power to give it back."

If truths regarding others are elusive on this foreign turf, truths about himself are equally so, and Adrian's quest necessarily leads to a self-evaluation that is fundamental to his identity. Adrian acknowledges that he is a member of the "lucky generation," those who, coming too late for Korea and too early for Vietnam, missed everything. Each time he questions the motives of the government or of Marcus or Sigmund, Maya dismisses his inquiry as naive, convinced no American can understand what being a part of such a country is like. Even Sigmund is out of patience with Adrian, accusing him of pretending engagement when he is merely a scientist observing specimens. For despite his efforts at participation, Adrian is finally only an observer, secure in his reputation, his wealth, and his smugness.

But it is Marcus who asks the critical question that demands that Adrian separate his personal self from his artistic self. In the early stages of their conversation, Adrian claims that he would react to the destruction of Sigmund's manuscript by publicizing this act of barbarism. Encouraged by Marcus's gestures to continue, he promises to go on national television and to bring the matter to the attention of the United States Congress. However sincere his original intention, though, his threats and promises sound hollow as the microphones become not merely a presence but Adrian's audience: Adrian is performing for the government, participating in a power play directed by the authorities. And if he cannot be anything but a contrived self under the archbishop's ceiling, can he be any more real even in the corridor? Marcus suggests that Adrian's concern for Sigmund's manuscript is really a concern for the story he is recording and creating:

He's been writing this story for you all evening! *New York Times* feature on Socialist decadence. . . . To whom am *I* talking, Adrian—the *New York Times*, or your novel, or you? (*AC*, p. 71)

Adrian does not know the answer. But the charge contains an acknowledgment of the theatricality that seems to be the only form of behavior possible in this arena, where rooms may or may not be bugged, where friends may or may not be trusted, and where writers may or may not be capable of living lives as something other than clinicians. Sigmund sums up the action in a comment that endorses Adrian's earlier reservation and makes authenticity impossible: "Is like some sort of theatre, no? Very bad theatre—your emotions have no connection with the event" (*AC*, p. 79).

The play's setting—a room with a four-hundred-year-old ceiling, styled in early baroque, with the four winds blowing through puffed-up cheeks and angels and cherubs holding up the plaster—adds a special contemporary irony to Adrian's efforts at understanding power. In this country, God has yielded to the Secret Police, figures of angels concealing the omniscient microphones that represent absolute power.

In such a world, it may well be unnecessary to write novels anymore—or at least to write traditional novels that imitate life. For the contemporary novelist, whose theorists bored Adrian at the Paris conference, the coherent, affirming form of mimetic literature may no longer connect with the real. But in such a world, where life itself is artificial, where the microphoned ceiling prescribes human action, art asserts itself as creative, not re-creative, power.

The novelists who assemble under the archbishop's ceiling approach their artistic commitments in special ways. Marcus continues to write in the realistic mode, but, as Maya observes, he can't write anymore. Sigmund insists on exposing the government, involving himself in literature as an expression of political discontent, but he is ineffective. It is Adrian, unsettled by the power of the microphones to reorder reality, who sees contemporary literature as a fictive construction no more or less valid than life. For, as Bigsby points out, "in the Archbishop's palace," which becomes, metaphorically, both literature and life, "there are no certainties; there is no touchstone of veracity, no proof of sincerity and authenticity." With the characteristic assurance and skepticism that define Miller's most recent work, *The Archbishop's Ceiling* offers searing commentary on the epistemology and the purpose of literature and on his own creativity and career.

12

▸▸

Contemporary — and
Vintage — Miller

In the introduction to *Collected Plays*, volume 2, Miller comments that, since *All My Sons*, which was written in the Ibsen tradition, critics have typecast him as a realistic playwright: "critics and commentators, like most of the rest of us, are lazy people, and once I had been labeled it seemed no longer necessary for them to look twice at the plays that followed."[1] No one reacting to Miller's work, however, should need to be persuaded that the playwright's professional career is a record of theatrical experiment and risk. As Miller rather modestly remarks, "The truth is that I have never been able to settle upon a single useful style" (*CP2*, p. 2). Though he has been underrated as an innovator of dramatic form, the fact remains that, after *All My Sons*, Miller was not content to create another realistic play. Speaking in his own defense, the playwright notes that "*Death of a Salesman* was not, of course, in the realistic tradition, having broken out into a quite new synthesis of psychological and social dimensions, and *The Crucible* was a work of another tradition altogether, and so on" (*CP2*, p. 1). At least since *A Memory of Two Mondays*, Miller's plays have assumed "metaphorical preoccupations" that, the playwright suggests, are "probably disguised for some by a design that asks for a realistic recognition of events and characters on the surface of a highly condensed interior life" (*CP2*, p. 1).

Whatever the measure of Miller's work, it is evident that critics have not responded charitably to the newer plays. Gerald Weales's review of the earlier version of *The Archbishop's Ceiling*, performed at the Kennedy Center, might summarize their response: "I will settle for the playwright of earlier days. Come home, Arthur Miller, and rediscover the American Maya."² Time will almost certainly modify the critical assessment of this play, which, as Christopher Bigsby suggests, deserves to become the focus of a critical revival, prompting theater critics and scholars to reevaluate the canon in the context of a major new phase of Miller's work.³

If such a renewal occurs, critics will undoubtedly look as well to *Elegy for a Lady* and *Some Kind of Love Story*, spare, two-character pieces, which, as a double bill, did not live beyond New Haven. Though these one-act plays do not rank with the intricately conceived and crafted *The Archbishop's Ceiling*, both are evocative pieces which, while portraying the tender side of human experience, further Miller's preoccupation with the nature of the real. Miller's prefatory note calls both pieces

passionate voyages through the masks of illusion to an ultimate reality. In *Some Kind of Love Story* it is social reality and the corruption of justice which a delusionary woman both conceals and unveils. The search in *Elegy for a Lady* is for the shape and meaning of a sexual relationship that is being brought to a close by a lover's probable death. In both the unreal is an agony to be striven against and, at the same time, accepted as life's condition.⁴

Elegy for a Lady takes place in a boutique, where an older man is searching for a present for his thirty-year-old lover, who is about to die. The two characters are the Man and the Proprietress, a young woman who offers not only gift suggestions but compassion and support. The tender relationship that develops between the two culminates in the Man's acceptance of an antique watch, which, he is satisfied, is a perfectly appropriate tribute. Together with the Proprietress, the Man rejects a number of ideas—flowers, a plant, a book, a bed jacket—and decides that what he wants most to say is "thank you." He settles, finally, on an antique watch, prompted not by some cruel impulse to remind her of her mortality but by the Proprietress's gentle suggestion that his lover "wants to make it stay exactly as it is . . . forever."⁵ The watch's enduring value will counsel courage.

The question of what to give sustains the dramatic action, but *Elegy for a Lady* subtly and suggestively questions more. Clearly the Man does not know for certain whether his lover is dying. He knows she is scheduled for surgery on the twenty-eighth of the month, that she has a tumor she says was diagnosed as benign, and that she has been in emotional pain. Often she would not answer her phone, and when she did she would sometimes leave the phone for as long as two minutes and, occasionally, allow a sob to interrupt the conversation. The Man has constructed a reality that may or may not coincide with the facts, and he has shaped the behavior of the previous several weeks, including his search for this final gift, around his belief that she has only a month to live. In his conversation with the Proprietress, he shapes and reshapes his story, trying to define the nature of the relationship with the dying woman and to understand his own feelings about her and about himself. The Proprietress's suggestions, not of gifts but of feelings, help him to create an understanding of how the woman he loves might feel about her own impending death, if indeed she is dying, and how he is responding to the coming loss. Gently, the Proprietress urges him into an acceptance of his recent exclusion from his lover's life, as the audience understands that the elegy may not be for the death of the lady but for the death of the Man. But if the circumstantial truth is elusive, the emotional truth is clear, endorsed by yet another teasing question, about the Proprietress. When the Man comes to understand that his quest may be a meditation on a loss having nothing to do with cancer claiming his lady, the Proprietress "embraces him, her body pressed to his, an immense longing in it and a sense of a last embrace." The Proprietress may be the woman, the meeting their farewell. As the Man takes the watch and chain, a gift from the Proprietress to him, she remarks, "You never said her name." The Man, starting to smile, responds, "You never said yours. (*Slight pause*) Thank you. Thank you . . . very much."

Some Kind of Love Story, the unpolished of the two gems, creates quite a different tone, preferring fast-moving, vulgar dialogue between a detective and a whore, but it explores the same issues as its companion piece. Former lovers Angela and Tom meet one night to discuss the Felix Epstein case, which Tom has been trying to crack for five years. Angela, he is convinced, has privileged information and holds the key to the innocent Felix's release from prison. But Angela will not tell.

The elusive quality of the truth rests not only in Tom's inability
to extract information from Angela but also in Angela's schizophre-
nia: the former prostitute, now wife to a man who beats her, is not
only a split personality but a multiple personality. She moves quickly in and out of alternate identities, thinking at times she is Emily,
an eight-year-old girl, Leontine, a house whore, and Renata, a respectable upper-class lady. Although Tom recognizes each of her
masks, he is never sure when he is seeing the naked self, never
certain whether to trust what Angela says. Yet his love for her
prompts him to believe even what he cannot confirm: though he
does not at first see the squad car that Angela insists is parked
below, he trusts his feeling that she is telling the truth.

The play proceeds as a kind of detective story, with Tom
O'Toole devoting his energies to freeing Felix from prison. On this
occasion, Angela has summoned him to her apartment out of fear
for her life, and she is prepared to tell him at least something of
what she knows. The details implicate the city's political guardians
in drugs and in conspiracy to conceal murder and suggestively implicate a network of criminals that could undermine the law en-
forcement of the country's major cities. But they also include confession of sexual involvement with at least three of the case's
principals, not to mention the detective. Tom's key witness carries
little credibility, only a biased ability to interpret, and more reason
to lie than to reveal. Yet after five years of silence, she provides Tom
with the clues he needs to pursue his cause.

If reality is elusive in *Elegy for a Lady*, it is equally so here,
where access to the truth depends completely on a schizophrenic
whore. Though the idea is provocative, Frank Rich is correct in
remarking that "it's hard to care whether the detective succeeds
in breaking down Angela or not: the complicated murder
story . . . never comes into clear focus, and neither does the heroine's potentially fascinating psychological make-up."[6]

Rich began his review by referring to the earlier staging that
year of *The American Clock*, a full-length play that had a somewhat
unusual production history before it reached Broadway's Biltmore
Theatre in late November 1980. The play previewed at the Harold
Clurman Theatre on 42nd Street, premiered at the Spoleto Festival,
USA, in Charleston, South Carolina, then moved to the Mechanic

Theater in Baltimore and, finally, to the Biltmore, where, despite repeated tryouts, it was a commercial and critical flop, closing before year's end. Rich noted that the two one-acters may well have been Miller's reaction to the failure of that "sprawling" full-length play, which "attempted to tell the story of an entire generation against a background as large as the United States map."[7]

Miller's dramatic canvas is indeed broad, ranging across the country as it chronicles moments in the lives of some thirty-five participants in the great economic and emotional tragedy that left stockbrokers splattered on New York City sidewalks and farmers begging for food. The play's narrator, Lee Baum, ranks the Great Depression as one of the two truly national disasters: unlike World Wars I and II, Vietnam, or the Revolution, it—and the Civil War—touched everyone. But the country held together because its people were believers in the American clock that would never stop.

As Lee flips through his mental album, he recalls the story of Henry, the Iowa farmer who, shamed into reclaiming his farm for a dollar and into a near lynching of a judge, moves east in search of labor. He remembers the young Sidney, who is urged by his mother to pledge himself to the landlady's thirteen-year-old daughter in exchange for free rent, and the Mississippi butcher who, though paid by the government to distribute meat, handed out maggots instead. In the Midwest, he met an unpaid sheriff who gave his radio to a black man in exchange for chicken dinners to impress his second cousin, who might get him a paying job. And in New York he met a man with a Gramercy Park address begging for food. The seventy-year-old Robertson, who shares the storytelling with Lee, talks of how he warned people to bail out of the market but to no avail. The shoeshine man, Clarence, who had forty-five dollars cash to his name, had purchased one hundred thousand dollars worth of stock ten dollars at a time, but he would not believe the man who carried thirty thousand dollars in his shoes.

At the center of this national mural of sketched-in incidental victims and depersonalized personal loss is the Baum family, with father Moe and mother Rose at its head. Lee recalls his childhood relief at withdrawing his twelve dollars from the bank just before it collapsed, his disillusionment at having the bike he bought with the cash stolen. He remembers the drama he and his father staged for the Welfare Office so Lee could be eligible for the WPA. And, with special poignancy, he tells of how his bankrupt father borrowed twenty-five cents from him and his mother gave him her diamond bracelet to pawn.

Miller uses finer brush strokes in creating Rose, who, accustomed to jewels and Park Avenue living, must move to Brooklyn and, finally, sell even her beloved piano. Played by Miller's sister, Joan Copeland, the character, though impressionistic, offers the narrator's one sustained personal memory, repeatedly suggesting the relationship between mother and son that persists beyond Lee's childhood and Rose's death.

But, finally, the play fails to move beyond its interest as personal and social history. As Jack Kroll remarks in his *Newsweek* review, "*The American Clock* never finds an effective dramatic shape: it's part play, part chronicle, but mostly it's Miller's last evocation of the images and people that have haunted him more than any others in his life." Similarly unimpressed, Clive Barnes suggested, "This Clock Is a Bit Off." Douglas Watt noted that "*The American Clock*, trying to tick away the past, simply doesn't work. The parts don't mesh." And Rich added his lament: "It's a bitter loss for the theater that *The American Clock* has arrived on Broadway unwound."[8]

Critics were similarly sour in reacting to Miller's recent one-acters, which were staged at Lincoln Center's Mitzi E. Newhouse Theater in a double bill entitled *Danger: Memory!* Though nostalgic over the fact that a Miller play (*After the Fall*) inaugurated the Lincoln Center theater program twenty-three years earlier, critics saw these efforts at combining the playwright's early concern with conscience with his more recent preoccupation with memory as, at best, footnotes to his playwriting career.

The mood of *I Can't Remember Anything* is autumnal. A two-hander in which aging friends (played by Mason Adams and Geraldine Fitzgerald) remember and forget their pasts, the play renews in its male character, Leo, Miller's irrepressible social voice. Recalling his commitment to communist causes, Leo now arranges to donate his organs to Yale-New Haven Hospital as a final protest against the American mendacity that his companion, Leonora, somewhat perfunctorily deplores. Leo's reviews of the past are only occasionally encouraged by Leonora, who prefers to remember as little as possible, seeking amnesia in alcohol. The conversation that constitutes this brief play moves through memories and present failings, settling always on the decay of American life. Though Leo energetically recalls the past and Leonora energetically represses it, the two share a sense of loss that gives this nostalgic piece its poignant flavor.

The second of the one-acters, *Clara*, is also a play about memory, though on its surface it is a detective story. Following the decapitation of his daughter Clara, who has devoted her life to social causes, Albert Kroll tries to recall and to repress the patches of his and her past that might give Detective Lieutenant Fine a clue to the identity of the murderer. That reconstruction of personal history, however, might also provide an explanation for Clara's vulnerability and ultimately attach moral responsibility for the murder to her father. Thus, recovering details of Kroll's liberal activism becomes a painstaking process for the detective, a painful one for Kroll. Through three mental encounters with his young daughter (only one of which was staged by Gregory Mosher), Kroll comes to understand that, as beneficiary of his social idealism, Clara has failed to proceed with caution in her work with rehabilitating criminals, one of whom is Fine's prime suspect. Kroll's acceptance of moral culpability might seem mere self-reproach, but it is of a piece with the Miller of *After the Fall* and *Incident at Vichy* and even with Miller's earliest work. For with Joe Keller, Kroll comes to understand that the tentacles of responsibility are everywhere.

Despite the inauspicious reception of his new plays—*Danger: Memory!* closed after thirty-three performances—the New York theater, both on and off-Broadway, has continued to be hospitable to Miller. The 1980 productions of *The American Clock* may not have succeeded, but clearly they reminded producers that vintage Miller might still work. In 1983 and 1984, Broadway's Ambassador and Broadhurst theaters became the respective homes for *A View from the Bridge* and *Death of a Salesman*, both with stellar figures—Tony LoBianco and Dustin Hoffman—in the leads. Off-Broadway's Playhouse 91 hosted a revival of *After the Fall* in 1984, with Frank Langella as Quentin; and a revival of *All My Sons*, with Richard Kiley as Joe Keller, opened at the John Golden Theater in 1987, winning the Tony award for best revival.

Off-off-Broadway, Miller's plays appeared at the Jewish Repertory Theater, in the form of a musical version of *The Creation of the World and Other Business*, and, at the Wooster Group's Greenwich Village space, in the form of fragments of *The Crucible* nestled in the company's production of *L.S.D.* And in 1987, *The American Clock* and *The Archbishop's Ceiling* both found homes in London, on the stages of the National Theatre and the Royal Shakespeare Company.

Miller's drama has continued to receive exposure in the legitimate theater, but even collectively these productions could not garner an audience so enormous as the one that assembled in the fall of 1985, in family rooms across the country, to watch *Death of a Salesman* on CBS television. Still hot from its successful Broadway run, the play, starring Dustin Hoffman, found an audience of twenty-five million, who acknowledged in Willy Loman—salesman, father, participant in the savage game of success—a range of coincidences in circumstance and character. Speaking in a *CBS Morning News* interview with Maria Shriver just prior to the airing on September 15, Hoffman described the kinship so many had with Willy:

As Arthur says, "this guy seems to be scratching on the glass, trying to get into the room of life and feeling that life is elsewhere," that we all feel a little like that, that we can't quite get into the mainstream: the terrible feeling of trying your hardest . . . and not really being appreciated for that value and instead seeing other people get further who are not as [long pause] honest as you feel you are in your work.

Forrest Sawyer, in his companion conversation with Miller, recognized in *Death of a Salesman* a "voice that cuts across time, continents, and cultures": the formula so simply identified—yet so painfully realized—of a classic.

Clearly, *Death of a Salesman* is Miller's masterpiece, but the artistic voice that refuses to be bound by time or space resonates throughout the canon, including the most recent plays. Contemporary critics following the fashion may dismiss Miller's drama as outdated both in vision and form, but, individually and collectively, the plays resist summary judgment. Moreover, the frequency with which they are being produced in New York and throughout the United States, in major European cities and on university stages—

not to mention Beijing—testifies to the playwright's remarkably constant reputation and catholic appeal.

Miller is in his seventies now, and he remains an energetic, socially conscious thinker and an accomplished dramatic craftsman. Not content to silence the voice that has defined American drama for four decades, Miller has recently completed his autobiography, *Timebends: A Life*, and he is at work on several dramatic works, one of them presently a one-thousand-page draft of *The Road Down Mount Morgan*.[9] America's best-known playwright may or may not have another Willy Loman in him, but productions of both contemporary and vintage Miller suggest that, at the very least, "attention must be paid." America's elder statesman of the stage is all too modest in summing up his achievement as having created "Some good parts for actors."[10]

Notes

1. Arthur Miller: Literature and Life

1. Record jacket, *Arthur Miller Reading from "The Crucible" and "Death of a Salesman."* (New Rochelle, NY: Spoken Arts Inc., 1960).
2. Arthur Miller, "A Boy Grew in Brooklyn," *Holiday*, March 1955, p. 119.
3. US Congress, House, House Un-American Activities Committee, *Hearings* . . . , Report No. 2922, 84th Cong., 2d Session, 1956, p. 20. Subsequent citations will be to H.R. 2922.
4. Arthur Miller, "The Shadows of the Gods," in *The Theater Essays of Arthur Miller*, ed. Robert A. Martin (New York: Viking Press, 1978), pp. 175–94. The essay originally appeared in *Harper's*, 217 (August 1958), pp. 35–43.
5. Miller, "A Boy Grew in Brooklyn," p. 120.
6. Miller, "The Shadows of the Gods," in *The Theater Essays of Arthur Miller*, ed. Robert A. Martin, p. 180.
7. Robert Sylvester, "Brooklyn Boy Makes Good," *Saturday Evening Post*, July 19, 1949, p. 98.
8. Miller, "A Boy Grew in Brooklyn," p. 122.
9. The situation recalls that of the Millers, who lost the family garment business to bankruptcy in 1928. There is a revealing error in the typescript that suggests the connection between Ben Simon, the older brother, and Miller's older brother, Kermit. On page thirteen, Miller inadvertently typed the name "Kermit" instead of "Ben." Kermit Miller stayed home and worked for the family while Arthur was at Ann Arbor beginning his writing career; during World War II, while Arthur, who was classified 4-F, wrote radio scripts, Kermit served as a lieutenant in the army.
10. The typescripts of *Honors at Dawn* and *No Villain* are in the Avery Hopwood Collection at the University of Michigan Library. The typescript of *They Too Arise* is at the New York Public Library. None of these plays has been published.

11. Arthur Miller, "University of Michigan," *Holiday*, December 1953, p. 143.

12. H.R. 2922, p. 29.

13. *The Pussycat and the Expert Plumber Who Was a Man* and *William Ireland's Confession* appear in *One Hundred Non-Royalty Radio Plays*, ed. William Kozlenko (New York: Greenberg, 1941), pp. 20–30, 512–21.

14. Jack Hutchens, "Mr. Miller Has a Change of Luck," *New York Times*, February 23, 1947, sec. 2, p. 3.

15. At that same HUAC hearing, it was stated that in 1943 he was alleged to have been proposed by Sue Warner for membership in the Stuyvesant Branch, 12th Assembly District, of the Communist Party. His alleged application number was 23345.

16. *That They May Win*, preceded by commentary on its purpose, appears in *The Best One-Act Plays of 1944*, ed. Margaret Mayorga (New York: Dodd, Mead & Company, 1945), pp. 49–59. The comment quoted appears on p. 47.

17. The version of the play referred to here appears in *Cross Section: A Collection of New American Writing*, ed. Edwin Seaver (New York: L. B. Fischer, 1944), pp. 486–552.

18. Arthur Miller, introduction to *Arthur Miller's Collected Plays* (New York: Viking Press, 1957), pp. 13–14.

19. H.R. 2922, p. 17.

20. Arthur Miller and others, "Should Ezra Pound Be Shot?" *New Masses* 57, 13 (December 25, 1945), p. 6.

21. H.R. 2922, p. 18.

22. Arthur Miller, "Grandpa and the Statue," in *Radio Drama in Action*, ed. Erik Barnouw (New York: Farrar and Rinehart, 1945), pp. 267–81.

23. In the *Daily Worker* of April 16, 1947, his name appeared in an advertisement of one hundred prominent Americans supporting the American Civil Rights Congress in protesting the persecution of German antifascist refugees, such as Gerhardt Eisler. On May 14, 1947, in the *New York Times*, Miller is reported to have auctioned off the manuscript of *All My Sons* for the Progressive Citizens of America. Also in the *New York Times*, May 25, 1947, his name appears as one of the sponsors of the World Youth Festival to be held at Prague, Czechoslovakia, under the communist-dominated World Federation of Democratic Youth. H.R. 2922, p. 13.

24. Introduction to *The Story of Gus*, by Arthur Miller, in *Radio's Best Plays*, ed. Joseph Liss (New York: Greenberg, 1947), p. 306.

25. Maurice Zolotow, *Marilyn Monroe* (New York: Harcourt, Brace, & Company, 1960), p. 95.

26. Arthur Miller, "Monte Saint Angelo," *Harper's* 202 (March 1951), 45; reprinted (as "Monte Sant' Angelo") in Arthur Miller, *I Don't Need You Any More* (New York: Viking Press, 1967), pp. 53–70.

27. H.R. 2516, p. 40. Many associates of Miller's were included in the list the committee compiled, including Armand D'Usseau; Isadore Schneider, the editor of *New Masses*; and playwright Lillian Hellman (H.R. 2516, pp. 40–48).

28. Zolotow, p. 263.

29. Ibid., p. 259.

30. Walter Goodman, "How Not to Produce a Film," *New Republic*, December 26, 1955, p. 13.

31. Mary McCarthy, in "Naming Names: The Arthur Miller Case," *Encounter* 8 (May 1957), 25, describes the manner in which the subpoena was served. The investigator, suggesting he could be helpful to Miller, as he had been to other writers and actors, casually asked Miller's opinion of Lee J. Cobb, leading him into agreeing that Cobb was a "great guy." When Miller agreed that he was, the investigator concluded that Miller would cooperate, since Cobb was among those who not only testified but named names. Self-satisfied, the investigator registered his surprise at Miller's not having been "rougher."

32. Richard H. Rovere, "The Monroe Doctrines," *Spectator*, no. 6679 (June 29, 1956), p. 877. Some observers felt that the HUAC treatment of Miller was more delicate than usual because of the possibility of alienating public opinion.

33. H.R. 2922, p. 14.

34. Ibid., pp. 23–24.

35. Arthur Miller, "Please Don't Kill Anything," *Redbook*, 117 (October 1961), pp. 48–49; "The Prophecy," *Esquire*, 56 (December 1961), pp. 140–41; reprinted in Miller, *I Don't Need You Any More*, pp. 71–77 and 118–165.

36. Miller, "The Prophecy," in Miller, *I Don't Need You Any More*, p. 146.

37. Clare Boothe Luce, "What Really Killed Marilyn," *Life*, August 7, 1964, p. 74.

38. Arthur Miller, "The Bored and the Violent," *Harper's* 225 (November 1962), 50.

39. See "The Literary Wars," *New York Times*, October 8, 1963, p. 37.

40. Louis Calta, "Arthur Miller Reading for His Lincoln Repertory Play," *New York Times*, October 25, 1963, p. 39.
41. Robert Brustein, "Arthur Miller's Mea Culpa," *New Republic*, February 8, 1964, p. 26.
42. Milton Esterow, "Arthur Miller's Play Generates Strong Controversy," *New York Times*, January 31, 1964, p. 14.
43. Barbara Gelb, "Question: Am I My Brother's Keeper?", *New York Times*, November 29, 1964, sec. 2, p. 3.
44. Arthur Miller, "Our Guilt for the World's Evil," *New York Times Magazine*, January 3, 1965, p. 10.
45. Robert Brustein, "Muddy Track at Lincoln Center," *New Republic*, December 26, 1964, p. 26.
46. Lewis Nichols, "In and Out of Books: Politics," *New York Times*, May 23, 1965, p. 8. A *Newsweek* article on the thirty-third annual congress held in Dubrovnik, Yugoslavia, in July, 1965, pointed to the political implication of choosing Miller as president of PEN: since Miller's standing in the Soviet Union and Eastern Europe was high, both as a writer and as a liberal, his presidency could well improve East-West literary relations ("PEN Pals," July 26, 1965, p. 92).
47. Arthur Miller, "The Writer as Independent Spirit: The Role of P.E.N.," *Saturday Review* 49 (June 4, 1966), p. 17.
48. Stanley Frank, "A Playwright Ponders a New Outline for TV," *TV Guide*, October 8, 1966, p. 8.
49. Thomas Lask, "Books of the Times: Mr. Miller Offstage," *New York Times*, March 18, 1967, p. 27.
50. Quotations in this paragraph are all from Arthur Miller, "It Could Happen Here—and Did," in *The Theater Essays of Arthur Miller*, ed. Robert A. Martin, pp. 295–96, 299–300. The essay originally appeared in the *New York Times*, April 30, 1967, sec. 2, p. 17.
51. Lewis Funke, "A Zestful Miller Starts Rehearsal," *New York Times*, December 6, 1967, p. 40.
52. Arthur Miller, "Topics: The Age of Abdication," *New York Times*, December 23, 1967, p. 22.
53. Walter Kerr, "Mr. Miller's Two New Faces," *New York Times*, February 18, 1968, sec. 2, p. 1; Clive Barnes, "Theater: Arthur Miller's *The Price*," *New York Times*, February 8, 1968, p. 37.
54. Arthur Miller, "Topics: On the Shooting of Robert Kennedy," *New York Times*, June 8, 1968, p. 30.
55. The widespread involvement of amateur and professional artists, writers, actors, and performers spread beyond the usual limits of

page and theater during the Vietnam era. In mid-August of this year, Miller read a sketch, "The Reason Why," at the trendy New York club Cheetah to raise money for the McCarthy campaign. The story is an antiwar parable about a man who, without need or reason, kills the woodchucks who eat a portion of his garden's tomatoes that he can easily spare. Harry Gilroy, "Writers Lift Voices at Cheetah Gala for McCarthy," *New York Times*, August 15, 1968, p. 34.

56. Arthur Miller, "The Battle of Chicago: From the Delegates' Side," *New York Times Magazine*, September 15, 1968, pp. 122, 124.

57. Ibid., p. 128. Miller, along with Martin Niemöller, Heinrich Böll, Rolf Hochhuth, Karl Jaspers, and Giangiacomo Feltrinelli, sent a letter of protest to Nikolai V. Podgorny.

58. There were, however, some who thought that Miller was too easily inclined to wave the flag of freedom without scouting the field. In December of 1968, Leopold Tyrmano, an expatriate Polish writer living in New York, strongly criticized both Miller and William Styron for their support for the Russian writer Yevgeny Yevtushenko. In a letter to the editor of the *Times*, Tyrmano attacks their naïveté in praising the Russian's courage and says they are misled by a person who is a counterfeit and not the brave rebel they believe him to be. "Yevtushenko's Career," *New York Times*, December 8, 1968, sec. 4, p. 13.

59. Francis Brown, "Miller Opens PEN Congress in France," *New York Times*, September 16, 1969, p. 43.

60. Henry Raymont, "Miller Refuses Greek Book Plan," *New York Times*, July 3, 1969, p. 29.

61. Inge Morath and Arthur Miller, *In Russia* (New York: Viking Press, 1969), pp. 7–8. A forty-two page feature article, "In Russia," by Arthur Miller, with photographs by Inge Morath, appeared in *Harper's* 239 (September 1969); it is an accurate condensation of the book.

62. "Sixteen Western Intellectuals Score Soviet Attacks on Solzhenitzyn," *New York Times*, December 5, 1969, p. 47.

63. "Brandeis Lands Two Generations in Arts Awards," *New York Times*, May 18, 1970, p. 38.

64. Quotations in this paragraph are all from Arthur Miller, "Banned in Russia," *New York Times*, December 10, 1970, p. 47.

65. Arthur Miller, "Are We Interested in Stopping the Killing?" *New York Times*, June 8, 1969, sec. 2, p. 21.

66. *New York Times*, February 28, 1971, sec. 2, p. 17. Novick's review

is "Arthur Miller: Does He Speak to the Present?", *New York Times*, February 7, 1971, p. D17.

67. Clive Barnes, "Stage: Miller Version of *An Enemy of the People*," *New York Times*, March 12, 1971, p. 26; Walter Kerr, "How to Discover the Corruption in Honest Men?" *New York Times*, March 21, 1971, sec. 2, p. 3.

68. Lewis Funke, "Miller—Before the Fall," *New York Times*, October 3, 1971, sec. 2, p. 1.

69. Arthur Miller, "Politics as Theater," *New York Times*, November 4, 1972, p. 33.

70. Arthur Miller, "Arthur Miller vs. Lincoln Center," *New York Times*, April 16, 1972, sec. 2, p. 5.

71. Arthur Miller, Review of "*In Hiding: The Life of Manuel Cortes*," by Ronald Fraser, *New York Times*, July 9, 1972, sec. 7, p. 34.

72. Tom Buckley, "Miller Takes His Comedy Seriously," *New York Times*, August 29, 1972, p. 22.

73. Josh Greenfield, "'Writing Plays Is Absolutely Senseless,' Arthur Miller Says, 'But I Just Love It,'" *New York Times Magazine*, February 13, 1972, sec. 6, p. 36.

74. Buckley, p. 22.

75. Greenfield, p. 36.

76. Buckley, p. 22. Miller's definition of religion is as independent and personal as one would expect: "There is no religion that is closer to a man than the one he invents, so I guess you can say in that sense that I'm religious."

77. Clive Barnes, "Arthur Miller's *Creation of the World*," *New York Times*, December 1, 1972, p. 28; Walter Kerr, "Arthur Miller, Stuck with *The* Book," *New York Times*, December 10, 1972, sec. 2, p. 5.

78. Arthur Miller, "Sakharov, Detente and Liberty," *New York Times*, July 5, 1974, p. 21.

79. Mel Gussow, "Arthur Miller Returns to Genesis for First Musical," *New York Times*, April 17, 1974, p. 37.

80. Ibid.

81. John J. O'Connor, "TV: Miller's *After the Fall* on NBC," *New York Times*, December 10, 1974, p. 91.

82. Murray Schumach, "Miller Still a 'Salesman' For a Changing Theater," *New York Times*, June 26, 1975, pp. 32–33.

83. Arthur Miller, "The Prague Winter," *New York Times*, July 16, 1975, p. 37.

84. "U.S. Urged to Guarantee Freedom of All Writers," *New York Times*, November 19, 1975, p. 25.

85. John Corry, "Arthur Miller Turns Detective in Murder," *New York Times*, December 15, 1975, p. 46.

86. Ibid.

87. Michael Knight, "Reilly Freed in Mother's Murder as Suppressed Evidence is Bared," *New York Times*, November 25, 1976, p. 26.

88. Clive Barnes, "Stage: Miller's *Crucible* in Stratford," *New York Times*, June 17, 1976, p. 31.

89. Israel Shenker, "Jewish Cultural Arts: The Big Debate," *New York Times*, January 13, 1976, p. 42.

90. Malcolm W. Browne, "Czech Police Hold a Dissident Writer," *New York Times*, January 11, 1977, p. 15.

91. "New Play by Miller Is Faulted in Washington," *New York Times*, May 3, 1977, p. 50.

92. Quoted in "New Play by Miller Is Faulted in Washington," p. 50.

93. Arthur Miller and Inge Morath, *In the Country* (New York: Viking Press, 1977), p. 167.

94. Arthur Miller, "'Our Most Widespread Dramatic Art Is Our Most Unfree,'" *New York Times*, November 26, 1978, sec. 2, p. 33.

95. John J. O'Connor, "TV: *Fame* Comedy by Arthur Miller, on NBC," *New York Times*, November 30, 1978, p. C22.

96. Thomas Lask, "Author Decries Casting of Miss Redgrave by CBS," *New York Times*, October 23, 1979, p. C7.

97. Fred Ferretti, "Critics of Redgrave Casting as Jew Ask Equal Time," *New York Times*, November 7, 1979, p. C30.

98. Janet Maslin, "Film: *Arthur Miller on Home Ground*," *New York Times*, November 4, 1979, p. 75.

99. Robin Herman and E. R. Shipp, "Notes on People," *New York Times*, March 13, 1980, p. C21.

100. Richard F. Shepard, "A View from a Bridge between Two Cultures," *New York Times*, March 29, 1980, p. 12.

101. Frank Rich, "Play: Miller's *Clock* at Spoleto U.S.A.," *New York Times*, May 27, 1980, p. C7.

102. James Atlas, "The Creative Journey of Arthur Miller Leads Back to Broadway and TV," *New York Times*, September 28, 1980, sec. 2, p. 1.

103. See Harold C. Schonberg, "Joan Copeland Remembers Mama—and So Does Her Brother Arthur," *New York Times*, November 16, 1980, sec. 2, p. 1.

104. John J. O'Connor, "TV: Vanessa Redgrave, Inmate," *New York Times*, September 30, 1980, p. C9.

105. Walter Kerr, "A History Lesson from Arthur Miller, a Social Lesson

from Athol Fugard," *New York Times*, November 30, 1980, sec. 2, p. 5; Frank Rich, "Play: Miller's *American Clock*," *New York Times*, November 21, 1980, sec. 3, p. 3.

106. Bernard Holland, "Arthur Miller Play Set to Stanley Silverman Music Resurfaces," *New York Times*, October 2, 1981, p. C3.

107. Leslie Bennetts, "Broadway Producers and Dramatists Lock Horns over Antitrust Lawsuit," *New York Times*, August 21, 1982, p. 17.

108. Ibid.

109. Mel Gussow, "From Broadway to Peking, It's Miller Time," *New York Times*, October 15, 1982, p. C2.

110. Frank Rich, "Stage: Two By Arthur Miller," *New York Times*, November 10, 1982, sec. 3, p. 21.

111. Frank Rich, "Theater: Arthur Miller's *View from the Bridge*," *New York Times*, February 4, 1983, p. C3; Walter Kerr, "A Play That Falls Victim to Its Author's Attentions," *New York Times*, February 13, 1983, p. H3.

112. Christopher S. Wren, "Willy Loman Gets China Territory," *New York Times*, May 7, 1983, p. 13.

113. Frank Rich, "Stage: Miller's *Up from Paradise*," *New York Times*, October 26, 1983, p. C22.

114. Jack Kroll, "Hoffman's Blazing Salesman," *Newsweek*, April 9, 1984, p. 107.

115. Eileen Blumenthal, "Liked, but Not Well Liked," *Village Voice*, April 10, 1984, p. 77; Douglas Watt, "Hoffman Shines in a Glorious Rebirth of Miller's Drama," *Daily News*, March 30, 1984, "Friday" sec., pp. 1, 3; Benedict Nightingale, "*Salesman* Demonstrates Its Enduring Strengths," *New York Times*, April 8, 1984, p. H11.

116. Samuel G. Freedman, "*Salesman* Extended Run Imperiled," *New York Times*, April 20, 1984, p. C3.

117. Michiko Hakutani, "Arthur Miller: View of a Life," *New York Times*, May 9, 1984, sec. 3, p. 17.

118. Samuel G. Freedman, "Miller Fighting Group's Use of Segment from *Crucible*," *New York Times*, November 17, 1984, sec. 1, p. 14.

119. Samuel G. Freedman, "Play Closed after *Crucible* Dispute," *New York Times*, November 28, 1984, p. C21.

120. Joan Barthel, "Arthur Miller Ponders *The Price*," *New York Times*, January 28, 1985, sec. 2, p. 5.

121. Edwin McDowell, "Publishing: Arthur Miller Writing His Autobiography," *New York Times*, February 8, 1985, p. C29.

2. All My Sons

1. In the introduction to *Collected Plays*, Miller speaks of the genesis
    of this play not in the contemporary incident but in a story told him
    casually by a Midwestern woman, a story of a daughter who, having
    learned that her father was selling defective equipment to the mili-
    tary, reported him to the authorities. Still, Miller sets *All My Sons* in
    Ohio, suggesting at least an awareness of the scandal. The incident
    is reported in Samuel B. Bledsoe, "Plane Defects Laid to a Wright
    Plant; Government Sues," *New York Times*, July 11, 1943, p. 25.
2. Arthur Miller, *All My Sons*, in *Arthur Miller's Collected Plays* (New
    York: Viking Press, 1957), p. 111. Subsequent citations will be
    given parenthetically as *CP*, followed by the page reference.
3. Miller notes in his introduction to *Collected Plays* that he had origi-
    nally conceived of Kate Keller as the central character and that her
    astrological beliefs played a prominent role. The original title of the
    play was *The Sign of the Archer*.
4. Arthur Miller, "The Family in Modern Drama," in *The Theater
    Essays of Arthur Miller*, ed. Robert A. Martin (New York: Viking
    Press, 1978), p. 72. The essay first appeared in the *Atlantic Monthly*
    197 (April 1956), pp. 35–41.
5. Miller, "The Family in Modern Drama," *The Theater Essays of
    Arthur Miller*, ed. Robert A. Martin, pp. 72–73.

3. Death of a Salesman

1. Walter Goodman, "Miller's *Salesman*, Created in 1949, May Mean
    More to 1975," *New York Times*, June 15, 1975, pp. 1, 5.
2. Arthur Miller, introduction to *Arthur Miller's Collected Plays* (New
    York: Viking Press, 1957), p. 32. Subsequent citations from the
    introduction and from *Death of a Salesman*, contained in this vol-
    ume, will be given parenthetically as *CP*, followed by the page refer-
    ence.
3. Arthur Miller, *"Salesman" in Beijing* (New York: Viking Press,
    1984), p. 238.
4. Miller, *"Salesman" in Beijing*, p. 245.
5. Sister M. Bettina, "Willy Loman's Brother Ben: Tragic Insight in
    Death of a Salesman," *Modern Drama* 4 (February 1962), p. 410.
6. Arthur Miller, "Tragedy and the Common Man, in *The Theater
    Essays of Arthur Miller*, ed. Robert A. Martin (New York: Viking

Press, 1978), pp. 3–7. The essay originally appeared in the *New York Times*, February 27, 1949, sec. 2, pp. 1, 3.

7. George Jean Nathan, "*Death of a Salesman*, February 10, 1949," in George Jean Nathan, *The Theatre Book of the Year 1948–49* (New York: Alfred A. Knopf, 1949), p. 284; quoted in Goodman, "Miller's *Salesman*, Created in 1949, May Mean More to 1975," p. 1.

4. The Crucible

1. Arthur Miller, preface to *An Enemy of the People* (New York: Viking Press, 1951), p. 7.
2. Robert Brustein, *The Theatre of Revolt: An Approach to the Modern Drama* (Boston: Little, Brown and Company, 1964), pp. 44–45.
3. Miller, preface to *An Enemy of the People*, p. 10.
4. Arthur Miller, *The Crucible*, in *Arthur Miller's Collected Plays* (New York: Viking Press, 1957), p. 245. Subsequent citations will be given parenthetically as *CP*, followed by the page reference.
5. This version appeared in *Theatre Arts*, October 1953; the passage quoted is from p. 54. C. W. E. Bigsby, in *A Critical Introduction to Twentieth-Century American Drama, Volume Two: Tennessee Williams, Arthur Miller, Edward Albee* (Cambridge: Cambridge University Press, 1984), reports (at p. 199) that a manuscript at the Humanities Research Center, University of Texas at Austin, dated September 1952, offers yet another version of this passage:

Oh, John, I have grown deep as a well; there are dark wisdoms in my soul I cannot even speak. But this I can tell you: all my life I felt a cramping cloud around my head; the world and I were hidden from each other—I was so ignorant!—When the women called me loose because the wind lifted my skirts up; shook a thousand fingers at me when a boy would call beneath my window—I would believe them and think myself an evil girl, and weep . . . And then . . . the fire came . . . I think of it always as a red, red fire, where we burned together, you and I. And out of it I walked, all new, and my ignorance was burned away. And I saw the truth as a December tree; those good and Godly women all hypocrites! Walking like saints to church, running to feed the sick and sit with the dying, and all the while pussed with envy for me; hateful they are and murderous, and oh so full of lies! And I cried out the truth, and God made men listen, and I will scrub the world clear for Him. . . . Oh, John, I will make you such a wife when the world is white again!

6. Accounts of the Salem witchcraft trials include Marion L. Starkey, *The Devil in Massachusetts: A Modern Inquiry into the Salem Witch Trials* (New York: Alfred A. Knopf, 1949) and David Levin, *What Happened in Salem?*, 2d ed. (New York: Harcourt, Brace and World, 1960).
7. Eric Bentley, "Miller's Innocence." *New Republic* 128 (February 16, 1953), p. 23.
8. Bigsby points to the similarity between Miller's response and Proctor's when each was asked to name names:

> MR. MILLER: Mr. Chairman, I understand the philosophy behind this question and I want you to understand mine. When I say this, I want you to understand that I am not protecting the Communists or the Communist party. I am trying to, and I will, protect my sense of myself. I could not use the name of another person and bring trouble on him. . . . I take the responsibility for everything I have ever done, but I cannot take responsibility for another human being.
> PROCTOR: I speak my own sins; I cannot judge another. I have no tongue for it. . . . You will not use me! I am not Sarah Good or Tituba, I am John Proctor! . . . I have three children—how may I teach them to walk like men in the world, and I sold my friends. . . . Tell them I confessed myself; say Proctor broke his knees and wept like a woman; say what you will but my name cannot—

9. Dennis Welland, *Miller the Playwright* (London: Methuen, 1979), p. 61.

5. A View from the Bridge

1. Arthur Miller, introduction to *Arthur Miller's Collected Plays* (New York: Viking Press, 1957), p. 47. Subsequent citations from the introduction and from *A View from the Bridge*, contained in this volume, will be given parenthetically as *CP*, followed by the page reference.
2. Arthur Miller, introduction to *A View from the Bridge: A Play in Two Acts with an Introduction* (New York: Viking Press, 1960), p. vi.
3. Arthur Miller, *A View from the Bridge*, in *A View from the Bridge: Two One-Act Plays by Arthur Miller* (New York: Viking Press, 1955), p. 106.
4. Ibid., pp. 158–59.

5. Ibid., p. 89.
6. Ibid., p. 93.
7. Ibid., p. 107.
8. Ibid., p. 109.
9. Ibid., p. 86.
10. Miller, "On Social Plays," in *The Theater Essays of Arthur Miller*, ed. Robert A. Martin (New York: Viking Press, 1978), p. 67. The essay first appeared as a preface to *A View from the Bridge: Two One-Act Plays* by Arthur Miller (New York: Viking Press, 1955), pp. 1–18.
11. The modified ending was retained in the 1962 film, in which Eddie stabs himself with a cargo hook. Norman Rosten wrote the screenplay, Sidney Lumet directed; the cast includes Raf Vallone, Carol Lawrence, Maureen Stapleton, Jean Sorel, Morris Carnovsky, and Raymond Pellegrin.
12. John Simon, "The Miller's Stale." *New York*, February 21, 1983, p. 52. Frank Rich, "Arthur Miller's *View from the Bridge*," *New York Times*, February 4, 1983, p. C3. Clive Barnes, "Miller's Powerful *Bridge* Finally Makes It to B'way," *New York Post*, February 4, 1983, p. 41.

6. *A Memory of Two Mondays*

1. Arthur Miller, introduction to *Arthur Miller's Collected Plays* (New York: Viking Press, 1957), pp. 48–49. Subsequent citations from the introduction and from *A Memory of Two Mondays*, contained in this volume, will be given parenthetically as *CP*, followed by the page reference. Miller may be referring to John Chapman, "Arthur Miller Grows in Stature; Van Heflin an Exciting Actor," *New York Sunday News*, October 9, 1955, sec. 2, p. 3; the review praises *A View from the Bridge* as "intensely, warmly written and acted in masterly fashion . . . a most exciting evening in the theater" but does not mention *A Memory of Two Mondays*.
2. Richard Hayes, "The Stage: 'I Want My Catharsis!'," *Commonweal*, November 4, 1955, p. 117; "*A View from the Bridge*," *Time*, October 10, 1955, p. 53; Brooks Atkinson, "Theater: *A View from the Bridge*." *New York Times*, September 30, 1955, p. 21.
3. Vivien Mercier, *Beckett/Beckett* (New York: Oxford University Press, 1977), p. 74.
4. Arthur Miller, "What Makes Plays Endure?" in *The Theater Essays*

of Arthur Miller, ed. Robert A. Martin (New York: Viking Press, 1978), pp. 260–61. The essay first appeared in the *New York Times*, August 15, 1965, sec. 2, pp. 1, 3.

7. After the Fall

1. Both plays premiered at the ANTA-Washington Square Theater, New York, *After the Fall* on January 23, 1964, and *Incident at Vichy* on December 3, 1964.
2. Arthur Miller, "Foreword to *After the Fall*," in *The Theater Essays of Arthur Miller*, ed. Robert A. Martin (New York: Viking Press, 1978), pp. 255–57. The essay first appeared in the *Saturday Evening Post* 237 (February 1, 1964), p. 32.
3. Arthur Miller, "Foreword to *After the Fall*," in *The Theater Essays of Arthur Miller*, p. 257.
4. Ibid.
5. Arthur Miller, "Our Guilt for the World's Evil," *New York Times Magazine*, January 3, 1965, p. 10.
6. Miller, "Foreword to *After the Fall*," in *The Theater Essays of Arthur Miller*, p. 255.
7. Ibid., p. 256.
8. Arthur Miller, *After the Fall*, in *Arthur Miller's Collected Plays*, volume 2 (New York: Viking Press, 1981), p. 181. Subsequent citations will be given parenthetically as *CP2*, followed by the page reference.
9. Early critics of *After the Fall* deplored the play's self-indulgence and its shameless glimpses into Quentin's—or Arthur Miller's—intimate life, objecting to what they saw as exploitation of Marilyn Monroe. Louise is recognizable as Miller's first wife, Mary Grace Slattery; Holga as his third, Inge Morath; other characters seem clearly to be modeled on people Miller has known.
10. Albert Wertheim, "Arthur Miller: After the Fall and After." In *Essays on Contemporary American Drama*, ed. Hedwig Bock and Albert Wertheim (Munich: Max Hueber Verlag, 1981), p. 20.

8. Incident at Vichy

1. Arthur Miller, "How the Nazi Trials Search the Hearts of All Germans," *New York Herald-Tribune*, March 15, 1964, p. 24.

2. Arthur Miller, *Incident at Vichy*, in *Arthur Miller's Collected Plays*, volume 2 (New York: Viking Press, 1981), p. 267.
3. Philip Rahv, "Arthur Miller and the Fallacy of Profundity," *New York Review of Books*, January 14, 1965, pp. 3–4.
4. Julius Novick, "*Incident at Vichy.*" *Nation*, December 12, 1964, p. 504; Henry Hewes, "Broadway Postscript: Waiting Periods," *Saturday Review*, December 19, 1964, p. 24; Robert Brustein, "Muddy Track at Lincoln Center," *New Republic*, December 26, 1964, p. 26.
5. Dennis Welland, *Miller the Playwright* (London: Methuen, 1979), p. 106.

9. The Price

1. Martin Gottfried, "Our Sometime Intellectual Superman," *Saturday Review*, September 29, 1979, p. 40.
2. Quoted in Ralph Tyler, "Arthur Miller Says the Time is Right for *The Price.*" *New York Times*, June 17, 1979, p. D1.
3. Arthur Miller, *The Price*, in *Arthur Miller's Collected Plays*, volume 2 (New York: Viking Press, 1981), p. 350.
4. Quoted in Tyler, p. D6.
5. Quoted in Tyler, p. D6.
6. Quoted in Tyler, p. D1.

10. The Creation of the World and Other Business

1. C. W. E. Bigsby, *A Critical Introduction to Twentieth-Century American Drama, Volume Two: Tennessee Williams, Arthur Miller, Edward Albee* (Cambridge: Cambridge University Press, 1984), p. 220.
2. Frank Rich, "Stage: Miller's *Up from Paradise*," *New York Times*, October 26, 1983, p. C22. *Up from Paradise* was staged in concert versions at the University of Michigan in 1973, the Kennedy Center in Washington, DC, in 1977, and the Whitney Museum in New York in 1977 before appearing at the Jewish Repertory Theater in 1983. *The Creation of the World and Other Business* opened on November 30, 1972, at Broadway's Shubert Theatre but closed before year's end. Dennis Welland, in *Miller the Playwright* (London: Methuen, 1983), documents some of the changes in this frequently

reworked play, comparing a 1978 typescript with the printed text of
The Creation of the World and Other Business (pp. 130–32).
3. Rich, p. C22.
4. John Simon, "Bronxward in Eden." *New York*, December 18 and
   25, 1972, p. 114.
5. Quoted in Samuel G. Freedman, "Miller Tries a New Form for an
   Old Play." *New York Times*, October 23, 1983, p. H5.
6. Arthur Miller, *The Creation of the World and Other Business*, in
   Arthur Miller's Collected Plays, volume 2 (New York: Viking Press,
   1981), p. 380.
7. Ralph Tyler, "Arthur Miller Says the Time is Right for *The Price*."
   New York Times, June 17, 1979, p. D6.

11. *The Archbishop's Ceiling*

1. Christopher Bigsby, "Afterword" to Arthur Miller, *The Archbishop's
   Ceiling* (London: Methuen, 1984), p. 93. Subsequent citations will
   be given parenthetically as *AC*, followed by the page reference. In the
   earlier version of *The Archbishop's Ceiling*, performed at the Kennedy Center, Washington, DC, in 1977, Sigmund is the protagonist,
   his letter to the United Nations the focus of attention; Adrian is
   excused from sexual involvement with Maya; and there is a critic
   present named Martin. A number of plot details also changed in the
   published version.

12. Contemporary—and Vintage—Miller

1. Arthur Miller, *Arthur Miller's Collected Plays*, volume 2 (New
   York: Viking Press, 1981), p. 1. Subsequent citations will be to
   CP2, followed by the page reference.
2. Gerald Weales, "Come Home to Maya: The Stage," *Commonweal*,
   July 8, 1977, p. 432. The reference to Maya connects with Weales's
   comment that "*maya* means the power to create illusions."
3. Christopher Bigsby, "Afterword," in Arthur Miller, *The Archbishop's
   Ceiling* (London: Methuen, 1984), p. 93.
4. Arthur Miller, "Author's Note," in *Two-Way Mirror: A Double Bill*
   (London: Methuen, 1984).
5. Arthur Miller, *Elegy for a Lady*, in *Two-Way Mirror: A Double Bill*,

p. 20. Subsequent citations will be given parenthetically as *EL*, followed by the page reference.

6. Frank Rich, "Stage: Two By Arthur Miller," *New York Times*, November 10, 1982, sec. 3, p. 21.

7. Rich, p. 21.

8. Jack Kroll, "After the Fall," *Newsweek*, December 1, 1980, p. 84; Clive Barnes, "This *Clock* Is a Bit Off," *New York Post*, November 21, 1980, p. 36; Douglas Watt, "*American Clock* Ticks Away at Past," *New York Daily News*, November 21, 1980, p. 7; Frank Rich, "Play: Miller's *American Clock*," *New York Times*, November 21, 1980, sec 3, p. 3.

9. Mel Gussow, "Arthur Miller: Stirred by Memory," *New York Times*, February 1, 1987, sec. H, p. 30.

10. Ibid.

Bibliography

WORKS BY MILLER

Plays

After the Fall. New York: Viking Press, 1964.
All My Sons. New York: Reynal & Hitchcock, 1947.
The American Clock. New York: Dramatists Play Service, 1982.
The Archbishop's Ceiling. London: Methuen, 1984.
Arthur Miller's Collected Plays (introduction by Miller, *All My Sons, Death of a Salesman, The Crucible, A Memory of Two Mondays, A View from the Bridge*). New York: Viking Press, 1957.
Arthur Miller's Collected Plays, volume 2 (introduction by Miller, *The Misfits, After the Fall, Incident at Vichy, The Price, The Creation of the World and Other Business, Playing for Time*). New York: Viking Press, 1981.
The Creation of the World and Other Business. New York: Viking Press, 1973.
The Crucible. New York: Viking Press, 1953.
Danger: Memory! (I Can't Remember Anything and *Clara)*. New York: Grove Press, 1987.
Death of a Salesman. New York: Viking Press, 1949.
An Enemy of the People. New York: Viking Press, 1951.
"Fame" (1970, unpublished).
"The Four Freedoms" (radio play). Typescript in Library of Congress, 1942.
"The Golden Years." Typescript in Hoblitzelle Theatre Arts Library, Humanities Research Center, University of Texas at Austin, 1939–40.
Grandpa and the Statue (radio play), in *Radio Drama in Action*, ed. Erik Barnouw. (New York: Farrar & Rinehart, 1945), pp. 267–81.
"The Grass Still Grows" (revision of "They Too Arise"). Typescript in Hoblitzelle Theatre Arts Library, Humanities Research Center, University of Texas at Austin, 1938.
"The Great Disobedience." Typescript in Hatcher Library, University of Michigan, 1938.

161

The Guardsman, Ferenc Molnar (adaptation) (radio play), in *Theatre Guild on the Air*, ed. H. William Fitelson. New York: Rinehart, 1947, pp. 67–68.

"The Half-Bridge." Typescript in Hoblitzelle Theatre Arts Library, Humanities Research Center, University of Texas at Austin, 1941–43.

"Honors at Dawn." Typescript in Avery Hopwood collection, University of Michigan, 1937.

"The Hook" (screenplay). Typescript in Hoblitzelle Theatre Arts Library, Humanities Research Center, University of Texas at Austin, 1951.

Incident at Vichy. New York: Viking Press, 1965.

"Listen My Children," with Norman Rosten. Typescript in Library of Congress, 1939.

The Man Who Had All the Luck, in *Cross-Section: A Collection of New American Writing*, ed. Edwin Seaver. New York: Fischer, 1944.

A Memory of Two Mondays [with *A View from the Bridge*]. New York: Viking Press, 1955.

The Misfits (screenplay). New York: Viking Press; Harmondsworth: Penguin, 1961.

"No Villain." Typescript in Avery Hopwood collection, University of Michigan, 1936.

Playing for Time (screenplay). New York: Bantam, 1981.

The Portable Arthur Miller (*Death of a Salesman, The Crucible, Incident at Vichy, The Price*, plus nondramatic writing), ed. Harold Clurman. New York: Viking Press, 1971.

The Price. New York: Viking Press, 1968.

The Pussycat and the Expert Plumber Who Was a Man (radio play), in *One Hundred Non-Royalty Plays*, ed. William Kozlenko (New York: Greenberg, 1941), pp. 20–30.

"The Reason Why" (1969, unpublished).

The Story of Gus (radio play), in *Radio's Best Plays*. New York: Greenberg, 1947, pp. 303–20.

"They Too Arise" (revision of "No Villain"). Typescript in Billy Rose Theatre Collection, New York Public Library at Lincoln Center, 1936.

Three Men on a Horse, by George Abbott and John Cecil Holm (adaptation) (radio play), in *Theatre Guild on the Air*, ed. H. William Fitelson. New York: Rinehart, 1947.

Two-Way Mirror: A Double Bill (*Elegy for a Lady* and *Some Kind of Love Story*). London: Methuen, 1984.

A View from the Bridge [with *A Memory of Two Mondays*]. New York: Viking Press, 1955; [two-act version] London: Cresset, 1957.

William Ireland's Confession (radio play), in *One Hundred Non-Royalty Plays*, ed. William Kozlenko. New York: Greenberg, 1941.

Other

Chinese Encounters, with Inge Morath. New York: Farrar, Straus, & Giroux, 1979.
Focus. New York: Reynal & Hitchcock, 1945.
I Don't Need You Any More. New York: Viking Press; London: Secker & Warburg; Harmondsworth: Penguin, 1967.
In Russia, with Inge Morath. New York: Viking Press, 1969.
In the Country, with Inge Morath. New York: Viking Press, 1977.
The Portable Arthur Miller ("The Misfits," from *The Misfits*, "Fame," "Fitter's Night," from *In Russia*, "Lines from California"). Harold Clurman, ed. New York: Viking Press, 1971.
"Salesman" in Beijing. New York: Viking Press, 1984.
Situation Normal. New York: Reynal & Hitchcock, 1944.
The Theater Essays of Arthur Miller. Robert A. Martin, ed. New York: Viking Press, 1978.
Timebends: A Life. New York: Grove Press, 1987.

WORKS ABOUT MILLER

Books

Bhatia, S. K. *Arthur Miller: Social Drama as Tragedy*. New York: Humanities Press, 1985.
Bigsby, C. W. E. *A Critical Introduction to Twentieth-Century American Drama, Volume Two: Tennessee Williams, Arthur Miller, Edward Albee*. Cambridge: Cambridge University Press, 1984.
Carson, Neil. *Arthur Miller*. New York: Grove Press, 1982.
Corrigan, Robert W., ed. *Arthur Miller: A Collection of Critical Essays*. Englewood Cliffs, NJ: Prentice-Hall, 1969.
Evans, Richard I. *Psychology and Arthur Miller*. New York: E. P. Dutton, 1969.
Ferres, John H., ed. *Twentieth Century Interpretations of "The Crucible."* Englewood Cliffs, NJ: Prentice-Hall, 1972.
Hayman, Ronald. *Arthur Miller*. London: Heinemann; New York: Frederick Ungar, 1970.
Hogan, Robert. *Arthur Miller*. Minneapolis: University of Minnesota Press, 1964.
Huftel, Sheila. *Arthur Miller: The Burning Glass*. New York: Citadel; London: W. H. Allen, 1965.
Hurrell, John D., ed. *Two Modern American Tragedies: Reviews and Criti-

cism of "Death of a Salesman" and A "Streetcar Named Desire." New York: Scribner's, 1961.

Koon, Helen Wickham, ed. *Twentieth Century Views of "Death of a Salesman."* Englewood Cliffs, NJ: Prentice-Hall, 1983.

Martin, Robert A., ed. *Arthur Miller: New Perspectives.* Englewood Cliffs, NJ: Prentice-Hall, 1982.

Martine, James J., ed. *Critical Essays on Arthur Miller.* Boston: G. K. Hall & Company, 1979.

Meserve, Walter J., ed. *The Merrill Studies in "Death of a Salesman."* Columbus, OH: Merrill, 1972.

Moss, Leonard. *Arthur Miller.* New York: Twayne, 1967.

Murray, Edward. *Arthur Miller: Dramatist.* New York: Frederick Ungar, 1967.

Nelson, Benjamin. *Arthur Miller: Portrait of a Playwright.* London: Peter Owen, 1970.

Weales, Gerald, ed. *Arthur Miller: "The Crucible."* New York: Viking Press, 1971.

———, ed. *Arthur Miller: "Death of a Salesman."* New York: Viking Press, 1967.

Welland, Dennis. *Arthur Miller.* New York: Grove Press; Edinburgh: Oliver & Boyd, 1961.

———. *Miller: A Study of His Plays.* London: Eyre Methuen, 1979; revised and expanded ed., *Miller: The Playwright.* London and New York: Methuen, 1983.

Articles

Bigsby, C. W. E. "The Fall and After: Arthur Miller's Confession." *Modern Drama* 10 (1967), 124–36.

———. "What Price Arthur Miller? An Analysis of *The Price.*" *Twentieth-Century Literature* 16 (1970), 16–25.

Epstein, Arthur D. "A Look at *A View from the Bridge.*" *Texas Studies in Literature and Language* 7 (1965), 109–22.

Gross, Barry. "*All My Sons* and the Larger Context." *Modern Drama* 18 (1975), 15–27.

Trowbridge, Clinton W. "Arthur Miller: Between Pathos and Tragedy." *Modern Drama* 10 (1967), 221–32.

Weales, Gerald. "All About Talk: Arthur Miller's *The Price.*" *Ohio Review* 13, 2 (1972), 74–84.

Wells, Arvin R. "The Living and the Dead in *All My Sons.*" *Modern Drama* 7 (1964), 46–51.

Yorks, Samuel A. "Joe Keller and His Sons." *Western Humanities Review* 13 (1959), 401–7.

Copyright Acknowledgments

Index

Index